Bible Stoı
Adult Ref

CW01460832

Bible Stories for the Reflective Heart

Illustration: R Vale (Procreate)

ISBN: 9798317207335
Imprint: Independently published

Preface

A Light That Still Shines

This book is born from many things — faith, memory, curiosity, and love — and at its heart is my late sister who always did (and continues to) inspire me. Maureen was a quiet warrior, a soul of deep conviction and wisdom, whose spirituality did not shout, but sang softly in every choice she made. Every challenge she went through, she met with courage. Paralysed after an accident at the age of fourteen, she could have turned inward with bitterness. Instead, she turned upward — with trust.

Her faith did not protect her from hardship, but it carried her through it with a strength that can only be called holy. Through her, I learned that true spirituality is not about having all the answers — it's about being there, fully present, with love and honesty, no matter the circumstances. She showed me how to listen for God/the Divine in silence, how to find light in the shadows, and how to keep holding on when it feels like everything is slipping away.

Her courage, her unwavering spirit, and her deep trust in something greater than herself continue to guide me. I feel her with me every day.

This collection of Bible stories and reflections is my offering — part tribute, part testimony. Writing it has helped me walk more closely with God/the Divine, just as she did. Her influence is woven into every page, not only as inspiration, but as a quiet companion on the journey.

Because of her, I keep writing. Because of her, I keep studying and seeking. And because of her, I feel called to keep sharing, believing that faith — like love — multiplies when we pass it on.

And my sister's faith was quiet but unshakeable — a lighthouse in the storm, not drawing attention to itself, but faithfully guiding. Even through unimaginable trials, her soul seemed to shine with a light that was not dimmed by suffering, but made purer by it. She taught me that spirituality isn't always found in loud declarations or perfect answers, but in steady courage, in love that doesn't falter, and in the peace that surpasses understanding.

Her way of seeing the world (with wisdom, acceptance and compassion; with trust in something greater) has become a map I follow. When I write, I hear her encouragement. When I study, I remember her thirst for meaning. When I share, I feel her beside me, reminding me that our stories matter – that memories matter – that hope matters.

She inspires me to keep going, not because the path is always easy, but because she showed me that God walks with us on it. Her life was a testament to faith that endures, and in that, I find the strength to keep writing, keep learning, and keep offering what I can to the world.

Each reflection in this book begins with a retelling of a Bible story, followed by thoughts for the heart or a quote inspired by my sister's faith in the Divine, and space for your own journalling. Though these stories are rooted in Christian tradition, they are offered with open hands and an open heart.

If you consider yourself religious, I hope you find echoes of your faith here. If you are spiritual but not religious – or simply curious – I hope you find meaning in the reflections, the questions, and the humanity of these ancient texts. Let the word "God" open gently for you; whether it speaks of Love, Mystery, the Divine, or the deep knowing within.

Wherever you are on your journey, may these pages be a quiet companion, a soft place to land, and a reminder that you are not alone.

Dedication

*For my beloved sister, **Maureen** –*
whose faith was quiet but unshakable;
whose strength was forged through suffering,
and whose spirit, even in stillness, moved mountains.
You taught me how to listen for God in the silence,
to trust in love when the path is unclear,
and to keep reaching for light, even from a place of pain.
This book carries your gentleness,
your courage,
and the echo of your prayers.
You are in every page.

Maureen 1963-2018

Contents

Introduction

"The stories we carry shape the soul."

There are stories in the Bible that many of us first heard as children—familiar names like Noah, Ruth, David, and Mary. Some we may have learned on our grandmother's lap or in a quiet pew on Sunday mornings. Others we may have discovered later, whispered to us in a season of loss, or read in awe under the stars.

But the gift of Scripture is that these stories are never finished with us. They deepen with age. They wait patiently for us at the crossroads, by wells, in deserts, and on mountaintops—ready to speak again, in new and needed ways.

For a time, I wasn't sure I believed in those stories anymore. My faith in God was shattered after an accident left my 14-year-old sister paralysed. After a strong religious upbringing, I kept asking: *How could a caring God allow a beautiful soul such harm?* For years, it felt like I was wandering in an emotional wilderness — questioning, searching, aching for answers that never seemed to come.

But slowly, through my (now late) sister's quiet wisdom, her radiant acceptance, and her deep spirituality, something began to mend in me. Though she suffered, her spirit shone with a grace that words can barely hold. She taught me, without trying, that we are more than our pain and that the soul can still sing, even from a broken body.

Gradually, my connection with the Divine returned. My faith grew stronger, deeper, quieter. And now, in my sixties, I know I am never alone. Even in the silence, I sense the presence of a Guardian Angel by my side. There is a divine companionship in life's quietest places ... whispers of love that never truly leave us.

You don't have to be religious to find meaning in Bible stories. These ancient narratives, whether read in the light of faith or from a more open spiritual perspective, still carry universal truths — about courage, forgiveness, love, resilience, and the human longing for connection with something greater than ourselves.

Being *spiritual* means you are attuned to the deeper layers of life — to wonder, to become aware of all aspects of yourself, to find compassion and search for purpose. It's about feeling that life has sacredness, even if you don't practice within the formal structure of a particular religion.

Bible stories, then, become more than doctrines — they become mirrors for our souls. You might not see them as literal history, but as timeless reflections of the human condition. David's struggles, Ruth's loyalty, Mary's quiet strength — these speak to the heart, regardless of belief system.

To be spiritual and appreciate these stories is to approach them with openness — to ask, *What truth lives here for me? What might this story awaken in my own journey?*

In that way, the Bible becomes less about answers, and more about conversation — with yourself, with the mystery of life, and perhaps with something sacred that words cannot name. In my reflections I will also be looking at the literary beauty and power of the words in these stories and considering these from many different perspectives.

Using This Bible Story Book for Group Bible Study

This book is designed not only for personal reflection, but also as a rich resource for group Bible studies. Each chapter offers a retelling of a familiar Bible story, followed by a reflection that invites deeper thought — not only about the characters in the story, but also about our own lives and spiritual journeys.

Groups can read the story together aloud, or invite one member to read while others listen. Scripture references are provided so you can read the Bible's account alongside the stories shared here.

The reflections that follow are written to open the heart and mind — they raise gentle questions and highlight spiritual truths that speak to the soul, whether you come from a deeply religious background or simply a place of quiet seeking.

Each chapter also includes a quote or prayer inspired by my beautiful late sister, offering a personal, heartfelt touch that reminds us of the strength and beauty found in faith.

At the end of each chapter, the *Journalling Invitations* section can serve as a prompt for group discussion. These will include both religious and spiritual/philosophical considerations. Participants can share their thoughts, stories, or personal experiences sparked by the questions — or they can quietly journal and reflect before sharing, depending on the group's comfort level.

Whether used in a church group, a circle of friends, or a spiritual book club, this format encourages open conversation, heartfelt reflection, and a shared spiritual journey — where all voices and experiences are welcome.

A "Sister's Light" reflects the strong bond I shared with my late sister. She was my beacon of support, guidance and love throughout life's challenges. The light she brought into my life was a source of strength and comfort. She would have loved sharing ideas, discussing, and planning this book. Through these pages, I reflect on how she continues to inspire me with memories of her wise words and guidance, and the strong sense of her presence that I still feel.

For the Spiritually Curious Reader

These reflections are rooted in Bible stories and Christian faith, but they are also written with tenderness for those who may not identify as religious. If you are someone who is spiritual, searching, or simply drawn to stories of human strength, mystery, and meaning, you are welcome here.

You may find value in the poetry of these ancient stories, in the questions they stir, or in the quiet places they invite us to explore within ourselves. You don't have to believe in every detail to walk through them. These reflections are not meant to persuade, but to open — offering space for contemplation, healing, and hope.

Where you see the word "God," feel free to listen for whatever name or presence speaks most truly to you—Love,

Wisdom, the Divine, the Universe, or even simply the still small voice within.

Let these pages meet you where you are.

This book is an invitation to return to sacred stories — not as we once knew them, but as we meet them now. Here, you will find retellings of Bible stories, followed by reflections meant to nurture the heart and soul. There is no heavy commentary here, just gentle thoughts, open questions, and room to wonder.

So come. Pour yourself a cup of tea. Light a candle. Step into the stories again.

There's more here for you than you remember.

And perhaps, this time, you will hear the whisper too...

Beginning Again: A Retelling of Creation

Genesis 1–2

Before there was time, there was nothingness and God. A great stillness stretched across the void, like a breath held just before a word is spoken. And in that holy hush, God dreamed.

Not of grand kingdoms or thunder, but of light.

"Let there be light," God whispered—not shouted, not demanded. A tender utterance, and suddenly — light spilled across the nothingness, warm and golden as the morning Sun on a sleeping face. It was not simply brightness — it was *goodness*, the very heart of God made visible.

With each new day, Creation unfurled like petals opening to light. Sky and sea danced apart, then land rose from the deep, cradling seeds in its belly. Trees stretched. Flowers swayed. Rivers sang. Each new thing pulsed with quiet joy, as if it knew it had been dreamed into being by Love itself.

God shaped the stars, not only to give light but to keep time so that we might one day learn to wait, to rest, to remember.

Then, on the sixth day, with earth still fragrant from new grass and the animals curious and unafraid, God bent low to the dust.

God did not speak us into being.

God *formed* us. Hands in the soil. Close. Breath held. Then — God breathed.

And we came alive.

Not merely as bodies—but as souls. Wide-eyed. Spirit-filled. We opened our eyes and saw... God.

And God saw us. And smiled. "Very good," He said. Not perfect. But good. Whole. Beautiful. Beloved.

Eve and Adam walked barefoot in the garden's quiet hush, the soles of their feet learning the earth, physically sensing the strength of the Universe. They listened to the rustle of fig leaves, the hush of water over stones, and the deep, abiding stillness in their own hearts. There was no shame, no striving, no fear. Only presence. Only trust.

And when God rested on the seventh day, it was not from exhaustion—but from a sense of fullness. The way an artist steps back, hands still dusted with clay, heart full of what has been shaped.

Creation was not only *made*.

It was *loved into being*.

Reflection: The Sacred Shape of Beginnings

Sometimes, we long for a fresh start. A clean slate. A second chance. And often we think we must earn it—fix ourselves, strive harder, prove our worth.

But the story of Creation tells a different truth.

That we began in love. That God delights in us *as we are*.

That our first home was peace.

That rest is holy.

That we were created not for perfection, but for presence.

No matter who or what you believe in, every morning, in its own way, is a new Genesis.

Every breath is borrowed from that first divine exhale.

Even in the midst of mess or sorrow, the invitation remains:

Begin again. Walk barefoot in the garden of your soul. Let God breathe life into you once more.

Journalling Invitations

1. What part of the Creation story stirs something deep in you today?

2. Where in your life do you feel the invitation to begin again?

3. Do you find it hard or easy to believe that God delights in you, just as you are? Why?

4. What does "rest" mean to you—not just physically, but spiritually and emotionally?

5. If you could walk with God in a garden right now, what would you say—or what would you hope God might say to you?

The Breath of Creation

"In the beginning, God spoke, and the world came into being. Light emerged from darkness, form from the void, and life from dust. With a single breath, humanity was given spirit."

Reflect on a time in your life when you experienced a new beginning. Was it intentional, like stepping into a new chapter, or did it emerge unexpectedly, like light breaking through the dark?

How do you see yourself as a co-creator in your own story? In what ways do your words, choices, or actions bring 'light' into the world around you?

If creation is an ongoing act, where do you feel called to begin anew today?

The Fall: A Retelling
Genesis 3

In the garden, peace had always reigned. It was the kind of peace that doesn't just sit still but moves in the air like a melody humming through the leaves; like sunlight playing on water. Eve and Adam had walked in the fullness of this peace, their hearts tuned to its rhythm. There had been no need for fear, no need for doubt. The world had been enough, because they had known their place in it: beloved; chosen.

They had plenty to eat and could eat from any tree in the garden but from the tree of the knowledge of good and evil.

But one day, Eve stood before the tree, gazing at its fruit. The serpent, more crafty than any of the other wild animals God had made, had spoken to her — a voice like a whisper in the wind. "Did God really say...?" Eve's heart fluttered, unsure. She had heard the words clearly, but the question planted a seed of doubt. Had God really said it? And if so, why?

The fruit looked ripe, tempting, just out of reach. *If only...*

And in that moment, a shift happened—quiet, subtle, but deep.

The thought took root: *Perhaps there is more to life than this. Perhaps the serpent is right and there is something that God is holding back from us. Perhaps if we take it, we will be more — more than just His creation. More than just loved. We could be equal. We could be free.*

And so she took the fruit, and with it, she tasted the sweetness of defiance.

But in her heart, there was no longer peace. Only the ache of something lost.

When Adam came to her, Eve spoke of the fruit, and her words carried the weight of the choice she had made.

It was no longer just about the fruit. It was about the world outside of God's trust. Adam stood with her, and in a moment of longing for something beyond the peace they had known, he chose to eat.

It wasn't that they didn't love God — they still *wanted* to. But they wanted more.

And when the fruit touched their lips, their eyes were opened. Not just to the beauty of the world, but to the sharpness of its edges, the weight of their own longing, and the sudden knowledge of *good* and *evil*.

They were naked. And they knew it.

They hid from each other.

They hid from God.

And in the shadow of the garden, where once they had walked with God, they now trembled.

Reflection: The Quiet War Within

The Fall wasn't just a story of disobedience; it was a story of *desire* gone astray. It relates to something deeply human—the longing for more, the hunger to fill the emptiness we sometimes feel inside, the desire to be something *more* than we are.

How often do we find ourselves standing before the trees of our own desires—wondering if we could have more, or if there is something we've been denied, just beyond our reach?

But the question is: What do we do with that longing?

Eve and Adam didn't fall because they were weak. They fell because they were human. And in their choices, we see ourselves reflected: our fears, our desires, our hopes for something more than what we've been given.

But God did not walk away. The moment they hid, God sought them. He came to them in the garden, calling them out of hiding. Even in their shame, His love did not fail.

And so, in our own aloneness, in our own times of longing, we hear that call: *Where are you?*

God's love is not only for the perfect or the unbroken; it is for those who wander, who fall, who hunger. And it is in the quiet seeking of His love that we find our way back to peace.

From a neutral perspective:
Reflection on The Fall: A Spiritual Perspective

The story of The Fall in Genesis is often seen as a tale of disobedience and loss, but from a spiritual, non-religious perspective, it can also be viewed as a profound metaphor for awakening, choice, and the complexity of human consciousness.

In the beginning, Adam and Eve exist in a state of innocence, a place where all is provided, and the world is without conflict. The Garden of Eden represents a time before self-awareness — before the mind wrestled with questions of right and wrong; before we felt the weight of responsibility for our own choices. But when they eat from the Tree of Knowledge, something shifts. They awaken to duality: good and evil, joy and suffering, freedom and consequence. They step out of unconscious bliss and into the full spectrum of human experience.

In this way, The Fall is not just about loss but about transformation. It is the moment we step into awareness; into the unfolding journey of self-discovery. The pain, struggle, and imperfections of the world outside Eden are not punishments but the conditions of growth. With knowledge comes accountability, and with awareness comes the opportunity to cultivate wisdom, compassion, and deeper understanding.

Perhaps Eden was never meant to be a permanent home but rather a starting place — a space of potential waiting to be realised. The Fall reminds us that enlightenment does not come from staying in comfort but from stepping into the unknown, embracing both light and shadow, and learning to navigate the beauty and complexity of life with an open heart.

Journalling Invitations
1. When you feel the pull of desire for something more, how do you respond? What inner voice guides you?
2. Have you ever experienced a longing that led you away from peace? What did you learn from that experience?
3. In what ways do you feel God's/Divine presence when you are hiding or when you are ashamed?
4. How might we learn to trust God's/the Universe's provision, even when our hearts are full of longing for something else?
5. When you are faced with temptation or difficult choices, how can you remember your place in God's love and trust His will for you?

Navigating Difficult Choices
Think of a time when you faced a difficult decision.
- What emotions did you experience as you weighed your options?
- What values or beliefs guided your choice?
- Looking back, what did you learn from the experience — about yourself, about life, or about the nature of choice itself?
- If you are currently facing a difficult decision, what would it feel like to trust that, no matter the outcome, you will grow from it?

Take a few deep breaths, centre yourself, and write freely. Let your thoughts flow without judgement.

Cain and Abel: A Retelling

Genesis 4

In the fields where the air was thick with the smell of earth and growth, Cain and Abel, the sons of Adam and Eve, stood before God, their hearts each offering something of their own as an act of worship. Cain, the older brother, brought the fruits of his labour — his hands rough from the toil of the land. Abel, the younger, presented the lambs from his flock, soft and tender as his heart.

The offerings were laid before God, with hope shining in their hearts and God accepted Abel's offering. Cain waited, expecting the same approval Abel would receive, but the fire of God's favour did not touch his choice of gift.

And Cain's heart, once full of pride, turned heavy. There was a tightness in his chest, a tightness that he couldn't shake. Why had God favoured Abel? What was wrong with his offering? He had worked so hard, poured himself into the land. Yet, something was missing — something he could not see.

And there, in that moment of bitterness, jealousy began to twist in Cain's soul like a vine reaching for the Sun. God, knowing his heart, came to him; not in anger, but in quiet grace.

"Cain," God called, "Why are you angry? Why is your face downcast? If you do what is right, will you not be accepted? But if you do not, sin is hovering at your door; it desires to have you, but you must rule over it."

But Cain's heart was heavy, and the words of God fell on ears clouded by resentment. Cain did not answer God's gentle plea. Instead, his heart continued to spiral inward, fixating on the unfairness of it all.

And so, later, in the quiet of the field, Cain invited Abel to walk with him. There, under the sky that had once been their home, where they had played as children, Cain's heart hardened. In a moment of brokenness, a moment of unspeakable pain, Cain rose against his brother. He struck Abel down.

And the ground, which had once borne fruit from both of their hands, soaked up the blood of Abel.

God, once again, came to Cain. "Where is your brother?" He asked, His voice full of sorrow, yet quietly patient.

"I do not know," Cain answered. "Am I my brother's keeper?"

The silence that followed was deafening. The ground cried out, and God's heart ached for both brothers: for the way Cain had chosen to cover his pain with anger, for the way Abel's life was taken by the hand of one who had once called him kin.

And though Cain was marked and cast away, God did not abandon him. Even in the consequences of his actions, God's grace still spoke, giving him a mark to protect him: an imperfect protection, but one that whispered: *You are not beyond redemption.*

Reflection: The Shadow of Jealousy and the Voice of Grace

Cain's story is one of the human heart's rawest battles: the fight between the desire to be seen, to be acknowledged, and the quiet seed of jealousy that creeps in when we feel overlooked. It is a story of sacrifice, not just of the material, but of the heart — of what we choose to give and how we give it.

But the real question is: *What do we do when we are rejected or when we feel that our offering is not enough?* How do we respond to the emotions of jealousy, bitterness, and brokenness that rise up in our hearts when we see someone else receive what we long for?

God's response to Cain was not rejection, but an invitation to do what is right: to rise above the crouching sin and rule over it. This invitation to master our emotions, to choose a better path, is just as real for us today.

Even in the midst of the shadow of jealousy, God's grace still speaks. His call to *come back to me*, to *make things right*, is never far. No matter the choices we've made, God is patient with us, seeking not to condemn us, but to redeem us.

Journalling Invitations

1. When you feel overlooked or rejected, how do you respond? Do you find yourself turning inward or seeking to understand the root of your feelings?

2.   How do you experience jealousy? How does it affect your relationships and inner peace?

3.   What might it look like to bring your offerings (whether it be your work, your love, or your heart) to God with a spirit of openness and trust, without comparison to others?

4.   What can you learn from God's patient response to Cain's anger? How might you hear God's voice more clearly in moments of inner struggle?

5.   In what ways can you offer forgiveness (first to yourself, and then to others) when you are hurt or when you make mistakes?

This story, like the others, invites deep reflection on the human journey: the internal battles we face, the decisions we have to make, the choices that shape us, and the ever-present grace that gently calls us back to wisdom and wholeness, no matter how far we stray.

))✦ *Handwritten Reflections* ✦)

You are invited to sit quietly with what you've read. Below is space for your own thoughts, prayers, or dreams that rise as you ponder these bible stories and their meaning in your life.

✏

✏

✏

✏

✏

✏

✏

✏

✸ *"The heavens declare the glory of God; the skies proclaim the work of His hands."* — Psalm 19:1 ✸
Let these pages be your sacred sky.

Noah and the Flood: A Retelling
Genesis 6–9

The world had become dark. Not just in the skies, but in the hearts of humanity.
The earth groaned beneath the weight of sin. Violence, greed, and corruption had spread like a sickness, turning what had once been good into something broken and bitter. The harmony that God had breathed into creation was slipping away.

And yet, in the midst of this unravelling, there was Noah. A man who stood apart; faithful, righteous, obedient. He was not a perfect man, but his heart was one that turned toward God in the quiet of the night, in the solitude of his work. God saw him. God knew him.

And God spoke.

"Build an ark," God said, *"For I will bring a flood to wash the earth clean. You, and your family, will be spared."*

Noah, with no sign of what was to come, trusted. He didn't question the vastness of the task or the strangeness of the command. He did not see the flood, nor hear the cries of a world about to break. He only saw the quiet, steady call of obedience, and he moved with it.

He built. Day by day. Timber by timber. Each hammer's strike echoed with faith. The ark took shape: a massive vessel that spoke of salvation, of protection, but also of grief. The weight of what would come hung over him, though he did not know when or how it would unfold.

And then, as the ark was completed, the flood came. Not as a storm of sudden fury, but as a quiet, unrelenting rise — a slow, steady drowning. The waters that covered the earth were not only waters of judgement, but waters of renewal. A cleansing.

Noah and his family (his wife, his sons, their wives) entered the ark with the animals, each one chosen; each one spared. The door was shut, and the earth was silent. The world that had once been was no more.

The rain fell for forty days and forty nights. And in that silence, in that dark, watery world, Noah waited. The days stretched on. The ark rocked gently on the waters, like a cradle, as the world outside became a distant memory.

But Noah did not waver. Even as the waters rose, he trusted. And when the floodwaters receded, and the earth was made new again, God spoke once more: "Never again will I destroy the earth in this way. This is the sign of the covenant I make with you."

And a rainbow appeared in the sky — bright and full of promise.

A symbol not of destruction, but of *renewal.*

A sign of grace. Of hope.

Reflection: The Quiet Faith that Bears Fruit

Noah's story is not one of grand victory, but of steady, quiet faith. He did not see the end from the beginning. He could not have known the full measure of what obedience would require. He did not control the storm, nor could he stop the flood. But he trusted.

Trust, like Noah's, is a choice. It is the decision to move forward even when we cannot see the outcome, to step into uncertainty with the knowledge that God's promise is enough.

In many ways, life often brings us into our own storms: times when the world around us feels like it's crumbling, when the floodwaters of grief, fear, and doubt rise up around us. Yet, even in these moments, we can find peace, much like Noah, who stood firm in the ark, knowing that God was holding him and his family.

This is something I learned through my sister's journey. In the darkest moments, when the waters of suffering felt overwhelming, she chose to trust. Even though the storm raged on (our hearts torn and questioning) there was an unshakable truth: God was holding us. We found peace in His presence, even when the world seemed lost. Through it all, we discovered that the promise of renewal was not just a future hope, but a present reality. We found peace through our belief in the Divine and in that peace, new hopes began to emerge, even in the shadow of sorrow.

God's covenant (whether you call it divine promise, universal truth, or a sacred bond) is not just a promise for the distant future; it is a promise for today, in the midst of every flood, every challenge. His rainbow still shines in our hearts: bright with hope, radiant with grace. Whether you believe in the Christian God or walk a spiritual path that respects all religions, this promise is part of everyone's spiritual journey. It is a thread of hope woven through the hearts of all who seek peace, renewal, and the restoration of what has been broken.

Journalling Invitations

1. In times of uncertainty or struggle, what does faith look like for you? How do you hold onto hope when the storm rages around you?

2. What promises from God do you cling to in moments of difficulty? How do these promises bring you comfort?

3. Like Noah, are there moments in your life when you have stepped forward in trust, even though you did not know what the outcome would be?

4. When you think of the rainbow as a symbol of God's covenant, what does it stir in your heart? What does it remind you about God's faithfulness?

5. How can you live today in light of the renewal that God promises — choosing hope, trust, and obedience even when it feels like the world is overwhelmed?

6. How have you experienced Divine presence in times of darkness or hardship? How did this bring you peace and new life?

This retelling brings us into the quiet strength of Noah's heart and the deep, abiding trust he held in the divine promise, even as the world around him was reshaped by loss and transformation. It is a story of renewal that speaks to the soul, reminding us that divine presence remains steady through every storm. This faithfulness is not just a story from the past;

it is something we can feel and trust in, even in our most difficult moments.

Abraham's Calling and Covenant

Genesis 12-17

Abram had lived a quiet life, rooted in a place that was familiar: his family, his land, the rhythms of his daily life. Yet there was something in the air, a whisper, a calling that stirred in his heart. It wasn't a loud voice, but a quiet invitation. God spoke to him, calling him to leave behind everything he knew: his home, his people, his security. The promise was simple, yet profound: *"Go to the land I will show you, and I will make you a great nation."*

The road ahead was unknown, but the message was clear.

Abram, though old and weary in years, packed up his life and began the journey. And yet, even as he followed God's command, doubt must have tugged at his heart. What did the future hold? How could he possibly create a great nation when his wife, Sarah, could not bear children?

Still, the call was there, and Abram trusted, step by step, even when the path was unclear. His faith was not a quiet certainty, but a faith full of questions. Would God fulfil the promise? Would he, an old man, really be the father of many nations? And yet, through every step, God spoke to him again and again, renewing the promise, reminding him that this was not a journey he would walk alone.

In time, God appeared to Abram once more and changed his name. He was no longer Abram, but Abraham, a father of many nations. The new name was a sign of God's covenant with him. God promised that Abraham's descendants would inherit the land and that they would be as numerous as the stars in the sky.

But even then, Abraham's heart was heavy. *How could this be?* He and Sarah were far past childbearing age. And so, when God told Abraham that Sarah would bear him a son, Abraham fell on his face, laughing at the impossibility of it all. *How could this ever be possible?*

And yet, God assured him: *"Is anything too difficult for the Lord?"*

Months passed, and despite the doubts, despite the fears, the promise came to life. Sarah, in the most miraculous way, bore Isaac: the child of promise. Through Isaac, God would fulfil His covenant, and the journey of faith would continue, extending through generations to come.

Reflection: The Faith That Follows a Call

Abraham's journey is one of trust in the middle of uncertainty; of stepping into the unknown with only God's promise as his guide. His story reminds us that faith is not always about clear answers or an easy path. It is about trusting, even when we don't understand. It is about holding onto a promise, even when it feels like everything in us is telling us it's impossible.

Like Abraham, we may face times when the road ahead is unclear. We may wonder how God's promises can be fulfilled in our lives. We may laugh at the impossibility of our circumstances, just as Abraham did. And yet, the story of Abraham teaches us that with God, nothing is too difficult. His promises are not bound by our limitations or understanding.

Abraham's faith did not mean he was free from doubt. It meant that, in the face of doubt, he chose to trust. And in that trust, God was faithful. His covenant, like a thread woven through time, continues to reach us today.

Abraham's story was marked not only by his physical journey but also by his ability to listen and respond to God's quiet voice. When God called him, it was not a dramatic or overwhelming command; it was a still, subtle invitation to step into the unknown. And in that call, Abraham heard not just with his ears, but with the deep places of his heart.

Hearing God's voice comes in many forms. It may come through an intuition that stirs in the quiet moments of our day, or through a thought that seems to arise from nowhere, urging us in a new direction. It can speak to us in the stillness of our soul, in the silence where our hearts are open and ready to receive. In these moments of reflection, God's presence becomes clear, not in a loud, commanding voice but in the soft whispers that draw us closer to what is good, what is true, and what is just.

Sometimes, we hear God through the language of the Universe: the patterns in nature, the unfolding of events, or the deep connections we share with others. These are the threads that connect us to something greater, the divine whispers that guide us, like the wind moving through the trees, invisible yet powerful.

For Abraham, God's voice was clear in the invitation to leave behind everything familiar. But for us, hearing God's voice may come in many different ways. It could be in the quiet moments of prayer, in the peace we feel after surrendering a decision, or in the unexpected wisdom shared by a friend. It is through these moments, big or small, that God calls us forward, just as He did with Abraham. And it is through listening to this quiet, intuitive guidance that we find the courage to step into the unknown, knowing that we are not walking alone.

God's voice is not bound by the ways we think it should come. It is present in the stillness of our hearts, in the rhythms of the world around us, and in the quiet confidence that we are loved and held through every step of our journey.

Journalling Invitations

1.   Have you ever felt called to step into the unknown, trusting in something you couldn't fully see or understand? What did that journey look like for you?

2.   When you face doubts about the promises God has made, how do you hold onto hope? What helps you move forward in faith?

3.   Abraham's faith was not a lack of doubt, but a choice to trust despite his doubts. How do you choose to trust in the midst of uncertainty?

4.   What promises from God do you hold close to your heart? How do those promises shape the way you live and walk through the challenges you face?

5.   Like Abraham, are there times when you have felt like God's promises were impossible? How have you

seen God's faithfulness in your life, even in those impossible moments?

6.   Abraham's journey began with a call to leave behind what was familiar. Is there an area in your life where you are being called to step out into something new? How might you respond to that call?

This retelling of Abraham's story highlights not just the external journey but the internal one of trusting God/your higher self. It's about the willingness to step out in faith, to hold onto promises/your intuitive feelings even when everything seems to contradict them.

Sarah and the Promise

Genesis 18:1–15; 21:1–7

It was hot, and the desert air shimmered around the tents of Abraham. He sat beneath the oaks of Mamre, where he and Sarah had long dwelled: wanderers with a promise, but no sign of its fulfilment.

One afternoon, three strangers appeared near the tents. Abraham, ever hospitable, ran to greet them, bowing low. He offered water, rest, and a feast prepared by Sarah's own hands. She, now in her nineties, moved quietly in the background, listening from the tent flap.

Then came the words that startled the air: *"I will return to you in due season, and your wife Sarah shall have a son."*

From behind the curtain, Sarah laughed to herself. Not a laugh of joy, but one of disbelief. *After all these years? At my age?* The ache of waiting, of longing, had grown too heavy. Her laughter was the sound of a heart both sceptical and tender.

But the voice of the Lord spoke, gently and firmly: *"Is anything too wonderful for the Lord?"*

And in time, the promise flowered into flesh. Sarah bore a son and named him Isaac — *laughter*. Her old laughter of doubt gave way to new laughter of joy. "God has brought laughter for me," she said, "and everyone who hears will laugh with me."

Reflection

Sarah's story speaks to the part of us that has waited so long for something, we've nearly stopped believing it could come. She teaches us that doubt does not disqualify us from grace. God meets us not only in our faith, but also in our fragile places, where the heart has grown tired.

There is something holy in Sarah's laughter. First, it is the sound of broken hope. Later, it becomes the sound of healing. Between the two is the mystery of a God who is patient with our questions and faithful to His promises.

Sarah reminds us that nothing is ever truly "too late" in the hands of God. Joy, even after long sorrow, is possible.

A Sister's Light
"She could make you laugh when you wanted to cry and somehow, it helped you do both. Her faith in the Divine wasn't loud, but it was deep, like roots that held even in storms."

Journalling Invitations

1. **What promises (or dreams) have you waited for in your life?**
Have you ever reached a point where hope felt almost too heavy to carry?

2. **When have you laughed like Sarah, out of disbelief, weariness, or surprise?**
What was hiding beneath that laughter?

3. **What would it mean for you to hear the question, "Is anything too wonderful for the Lord?"**
How does it stir your heart today?

4. **Where in your life might God be quietly working, even when you feel nothing is changing?**
What unseen seeds might be growing?

5. **Sarah named her joy 'Isaac' — laughter.**
If a long-awaited joy came to you, what name might you give it?

6. **How do you relate to the idea that God honours even faltering faith?**
Can you recall a time when you felt God's presence despite your doubts?

7. **What kind of laughter do you long for now — the laughter of joy, release, reunion, healing?**
What might help make space for that laughter to rise again?

We turn now to Hagar's story, a woman often overlooked, yet seen so clearly by God. Her story is a one of exile, resilience and divine tenderness.

Hagar in the Wilderness
Genesis 16:1–14; 21:8–21

The desert wind was harsh, and so was the life Hagar had
been given. She was not chosen like Sarah, not called like
Abraham. She was an Egyptian servant, drawn into a story not
her own — asked to bear a child for someone else's promise.

For Sarai (Abraham's wife) longed for a child. She had
heard God's promise to her husband Abram (that his
descendants would be as countless as the stars) but time had
passed, and her womb remained empty. The ache of waiting
grew heavier with every season.

So Sarai did what many women of her time might have
done in desperation: she gave her Egyptian servant, Hagar, to
Abram, hoping to bear a child through her. Hagar, with no
voice in the matter, became pregnant.

But with the child growing within her, Hagar began to see
herself differently; no longer just a servant, but a woman,
about to become a mother. Tension flared between the two
women. Sarai, feeling cast aside and wounded, treated Hagar
harshly. So Hagar fled into the wilderness, alone, afraid, and
carrying new life.

In that desolate place, an angel of the Lord found her near a
spring. The angel called her by name: *"Hagar, servant of
Sarai, where have you come from, and where are you going?"*
He listened to her sorrow and gave her a message of hope. She
would bear a son, and his name would be Ishmael, meaning
"God hears."

Overcome, Hagar gave a name to God — *El Roi*, "the God
who sees me." She said, *"I have now seen the One who sees
me."*

Years later, after Sarai (now Sarah) finally bore a son of her
own, tensions rose again. Hagar and Ishmael were sent away
into the wilderness once more. But God did not forget them.
When their water ran out and Hagar wept, God heard her
son's cries and opened her eyes to a nearby well. ... Life, where
there had seemed to be only death.

The boy grew strong, and God remained with them. And Hagar, the outcast, became the first person in Scripture to give God a name: **El Roi:** *The God who sees me.*

Reflection

Hagar's story is not an easy one. She was not asked if she wanted to bear a child; the decision was made for her. Yet in her pain, confusion, and isolation, something extraordinary happened: God *saw* her.

Hagar is the first person in the Bible to name God — and the name she gives is full of wonder and intimacy: *El Roi*, "the God who sees me." This name springs not from triumph but from abandonment. It is in her lowest moment, in the wilderness, that she is most deeply seen.

Many of us have wilderness seasons: times when we feel invisible, misunderstood, or used. Hagar's story whispers that we are not alone. God sees us. Even when others forget us, even when the journey is not what we would have chosen, there is a wellspring of grace hidden nearby.

We may not always get to choose the paths we walk, but like Hagar, we can discover that even in hard places, God is near.

Hagar's story is not one of grand triumphs or bold callings, but of survival in the margins, and that, too, is sacred. She shows us that even when we feel forgotten by the world, we are seen by God. Not generically, not as part of someone else's story, but by name, by heart.

There are times we cannot see the path ahead, when sorrow presses too close. But like Hagar, we are not abandoned. Sometimes, the well has always been there — we just need eyes to see it.

She reminds us that the wilderness can become a place of revelation. Even when we don't know where we are going, God meets us with the question: *Where have you come from, and where are you going?* And gently, a spring begins to flow.

For those who are grieving ...

Hagar was cast into the wilderness, but she was not truly alone. In her despair, God saw her and spoke to her in a way that assured her of divine presence and care. This is not unlike grief. When someone we love deeply is no longer physically with us, we are thrust into a kind of wilderness — disoriented, aching, searching for where love goes after death.

And yet... like Hagar at the spring, there are moments when we feel something stir in the stillness. A breeze that carries memory. A dream that comforts. A word or song that arrives just when we need it. These are the quiet ways we are *seen* — and maybe, just maybe, our loved ones are part of that seeing.

Hagar named God *El Roi* — the One who sees. And perhaps, in a mysterious way, the ones we've loved and lost are still seen by that same God — and still *see us*, too. When we sense their nearness, it may be because love is not bounded by the veil of death. It lingers in presence, in memory, in spirit.

So when you sense your loved one close (in a moment of peace or in a sudden quiet joy) trust that like Hagar, you are not forgotten. You are seen. And perhaps, just as Hagar once whispered God's name in the wilderness, they now whisper yours, softly, from the other side.

For Those we Still Feel Close to

A personal reflection inspired by Hagar's story

When I read Hagar's story, I see a woman who was cast out and yet not abandoned; a woman who met God in her loneliness and came to know Him as *El Roi*, the God who sees.

There is something about that moment — alone by the spring, full of sorrow, and suddenly aware of divine presence — that touches a place in me I cannot quite name. It reminds me of grief. Of how, even after someone we love is gone, there are moments when their presence quietly brushes against our lives.

I have felt that with my sister.

Though she is no longer here in body, there are days I feel her near. In dreams. In the way light falls through the trees. In the silence, when I need wisdom and suddenly remember something she once said — as if she's just whispered it again.

Grief can feel like a wilderness. But Hagar's story tells me that the wilderness is not God-forsaken. It is God-filled. Just as she was seen and comforted, I believe my sister is still held by that same seeing God; and somehow, I am still held by her love too.

Maybe the veil between this world and the next is thinner than we know. Maybe when we feel the presence of those we've lost, it's not wishful thinking. Maybe it's a kind of spring in the desert — quiet, life-giving, and deeply real.

A Sister's Whispered Prayer

"May you feel the eyes of heaven upon you, even when the world turns away.
May you find a well where you thought there was only sand.
May your tears be heard, as mine were.
You are never alone."

Journalling Invitations

1. **When have you felt unseen, overlooked, or forgotten?**
What helped you find your way back to yourself?

2. **Hagar named God as the One who sees her.**
How do you most long to be seen—by God, by others, by yourself?

3. **Are there places in your life right now that feel like wilderness?**
Where might God/the Divine be meeting you, even there?

4. **What is your "spring in the desert"?**
A source of quiet strength, beauty, or hope that sustains you unexpectedly?

5. **"Where have you come from, and where are you going?"**
How would you answer those questions today?

6. **What might it mean to name your pain honestly, as Hagar did, while still moving forward with courage?**

The Binding of Isaac

Genesis 22:1–19

The Sun rose slowly on a day that would test the soul of Abraham. God called to him, and he answered, as always, "Here I am." But the command that followed shook the very foundation of the promise:

"Take your son, your only son Isaac, whom you love... and offer him as a burnt offering."

Isaac (the laughter of Sarah, the miracle of old age, the fulfilment of hope) was now to be placed on an altar.

Early the next morning, Abraham saddled the donkey and set out. For three days, he journeyed with his son. He said little. Isaac, sensing the silence, asked gently, "Father, we have the fire and the wood — but where is the lamb?"

Abraham replied, "God will provide."

Atop Mount Moriah, he built an altar. He bound Isaac and laid him there. And as he reached for the knife, a voice called out, "Abraham, Abraham!" He stopped. A ram had appeared, caught in the thicket.

Isaac was spared. The altar held not the child of promise, but the offering God had provided.

Abraham named the place *Yahweh Yireh* — **"The Lord will provide."**

Reflection

This story holds deep mystery. It asks us to sit with questions that may not resolve easily. But at its heart is something universal: the struggle to trust when the path makes no sense.

Abraham trusted in a promise he could not yet see. Isaac trusted his father as they walked together. And in the end, God revealed a way through when all hope seemed lost.

Perhaps this story reminds us that faith is not the absence of struggle, but the willingness to walk forward even when we do not understand. And that sometimes, the provision comes only *after* we have climbed the mountain.

God sees. God provides. Even in the hardest places.

From a neutral perspective:
The story of the Binding of Isaac is one of tension—between trust and fear, duty and love, destiny and choice. It forces us to ask: What do we hold most dear, and what are we willing to risk in pursuit of something greater than ourselves?

At its core, this is a story about the weight of sacrifice and the uncertainty of faith; not just in a higher power, but in life itself. There are moments when we stand at the edge of an unknown path, heart pounding, uncertain if the ground will hold beneath us. Like Isaac, we may feel powerless in the hands of forces beyond our control. Like Abraham, we may struggle with choices that seem impossible.

Yet, the story also reminds us that just when all seems lost, there is often another way forward; one we cannot yet see. Perhaps the lesson is not in obedience, but in trust: trust that we are not alone in our hardest moments, trust that there is meaning beyond the trial, and trust that even at the last moment, something unexpected may appear to change everything.

A Quote by My Sister's Spirit
"She understood sacrifice; not just in grand gestures, but in quiet, everyday ways. She gave when it cost her, but she never made you feel the weight of it. Her trust in God/the Divine was steady, even when life wasn't fair."

Journalling Invitations

1. **What are you holding right now that feels too precious, too fragile, to surrender?**
What would it mean to place it gently into God's hands or the hands of your Angels?

2. **"God will provide," Abraham said, without knowing how.**
What in your life is calling for that kind of trust?

3. **Have you ever climbed a personal 'Mount Moriah' ... a place of testing or fear?**

What did you discover there about God, the Divine, or about yourself?

4. **What does it mean to you that God intervened and provided another way?**
How have you experienced unexpected provision?

5. **How do you reconcile faith with the presence of pain, mystery, or unanswered questions?**
What comforts or challenges you in this story?

6. **Like the experiences I have shared with my sister, is there someone in your life who, like Isaac, walked with quiet trust?**
What did their presence teach you about courage or love?

Rebekah at the Well ... a story of divine guidance and unexpected beginnings
Genesis 24:1–67

Abraham, now very old, longed to find a wife for his son Isaac — not from among the Canaanites, but from his own people. So he sent his trusted servant on a long journey northward, back to the land of his kin, carrying gifts and a prayer.

When the servant reached the town of Nahor, he stopped at a well, the meeting place of women and water and everyday life. He prayed silently, "Let the woman who offers water not just to me, but to my camels also, be the one You have chosen."

Before he had finished praying, a young woman appeared. Her name was Rebekah. She was kind and strong, graceful and generous. Without hesitation, she gave him water—and then drew for the camels too, until they were satisfied.

The servant watched in wonder. His prayer had barely taken breath, and the answer had arrived.

Rebekah listened to his story. She invited him into her family's home and, in time, agreed to leave all she knew to journey to a land she had never seen, to marry a man she had never met.

As she approached Isaac in the field, he looked up and saw her coming. She veiled herself. He took her into his mother Sarah's tent, and she became his wife. And Isaac was comforted after his mother's death.

Reflection
Rebekah's story is one of quiet courage. She did not perform a miracle or lead a nation, but she said yes when the moment came, and that yes changed everything.

Sometimes, guidance arrives like it did at the well: in ordinary moments, through small acts of kindness, in the flow of daily life. And sometimes, the next step asks for great trust.

Rebekah reminds us that faith often looks like openness. Her hospitality became holy. Her journey, though uncertain, was guided. She shows us that God is present not only on the mountaintop, but also by the well, where prayers are whispered, and answers come with grace.

Abraham's Intuitive Guidance: Abraham didn't tell his servant exactly *who* to choose. Instead, he gave a broad instruction: *find a wife for Isaac from among my kindred.* And then entrusted the rest to God and to the servant's listening heart.

His trust ran deeper than logic or control. He released the outcome and relied on the discernment of his servant (who then prayed his own heartfelt prayer); the leading of the Spirit in the flow of life (meeting at a well, where people naturally gathered) and a sign rooted in character, not appearances—a woman who would show kindness, not only to a stranger, but to his animals.

The sign itself — "Let her offer water to me *and* my camels" — was a gesture not easily performed. To draw water for ten camels was no small act. It required time, strength, and generous willingness.

What's striking is this: Abraham trusted the unknown. He trusted that *when the right person appeared*, something in the situation would resonate with peace, purpose, and providence. And his servant trusted that *his prayer would be heard*, and that he'd recognise the answer not by thunder or fire, but through the intuition of grace in ordinary actions.

A Sister's Light
"There was a gentleness to her strength, and you always left her feeling lighter. She didn't need to know where the road would end; she just trusted the One who walked with her."

Journalling Invitations

1. **Have you ever experienced an answer to prayer that came quietly, like Rebekah at the well?**
What did it teach you about listening or noticing?

2. **What does hospitality mean to you, not just in your home, but in your heart?**
How do you make space for others?

3. **Have you ever been called to say "yes" to something before seeing the whole picture?**
What helped you trust the journey?

4. **Rebekah drew water for the camels without being asked.**
What simple acts of kindness have left a lasting impression on you?

5. **Where in your life might God be guiding gently, through ordinary things?**
What wells are you drawing from these days?

6. **Is there someone whose quiet courage reminds you of Rebekah?**
How might their example inspire your own path?

7. When have you, like Abraham, handed over something deeply important and trusted God/the Divine to lead through intuition, prayer, and the quiet wisdom of others?

8. Are there decisions you are facing where you feel invited to listen more deeply; not just to logic, but to the "still small voice" within?

Jacob's Dream at Bethel ...

Now, we journey with Jacob, the dreamer, the wanderer, the one caught between past and future. His story at Bethel is one of transformation; a sacred moment when the veil between earth and heaven is drawn back.
Genesis 28:10–22

Jacob is a key figure in the Bible, known as one of the patriarchs of Israel. He was the son of Isaac and Rebekah and the twin brother of Esau. Jacob's name, which means "supplanter" or "he grasps the heel," reflects his complicated relationship with his brother. He is known for obtaining Esau's birthright and blessing through cleverness and deception.

Jacob was on the run. Having deceived his brother Esau and taken his blessing, he fled from home, uncertain of what lay ahead. The Sun was setting as he reached a lonely stretch of land, and with only a stone for a pillow, Jacob lay down under the stars.

That night, he dreamed.

A ladder stretched from the earth up into heaven. Angels were ascending and descending upon it. And there, above it all, stood the Lord, who spoke:

"I am the Lord, the God of Abraham and Isaac. I am with you. I will watch over you wherever you go."

Jacob awoke in awe. The wilderness had become a sanctuary.

"Surely the Lord is in this place, and I did not know it."

He took the stone he had used for a pillow and set it upright as a pillar. He poured oil over it and named the place *Bethel* — "House of God."

What began as a place of fear became a place of blessing. God met Jacob not in perfection, but in flight, fatigue, and failure. And that became holy ground.

Later, in a wrestling match with a mysterious being (next story) — often understood as an angel or God Himself — Jacob is given a new name, **Israel**, meaning "he struggles with God." This signifies his perseverance and the covenant promise through him.

Jacob fathers twelve sons who become the heads of the twelve tribes of Israel. His story is one of growth, reconciliation, and the unfolding of God's plan despite human flaws.

Reflection

Jacob wasn't looking for God; he was looking for escape. And yet, even in that weary, uncertain place, **God found him.** Not to punish or scold, but to offer presence, promise, and peace.

Jacob's life is marked by a deep spiritual journey. After fleeing his brother's anger, he has a transformative encounter with God in a dream at Bethel, where he sees a ladder reaching to heaven

His story, a gentle reminder: we don't have to be perfect to be met by grace. We don't have to be ready, or worthy, or even awake to the sacredness around us. Sometimes God speaks when we are at our lowest, our loneliest; when we have only stones beneath our heads and regrets in our hearts.

And when that voice comes, it does not always change our circumstances, but it changes *us*. It reminds us we are not alone. That even the barren places can become holy. That the journey we're on, however crooked, is still wrapped in promise.

A Quote inspired by memories with my sister ...

"She never pretended to be perfect. That's what made her feel so safe. She had wrestled with life, with pain, with questions; and still, she believed. Her faith felt like a shelter, not a spotlight. She taught me that God/the Divine Spirit meets us exactly where we are."

Journalling Invitations

1. **Have you ever had a "Bethel" moment: a time when you realised God was with you, even**

when you hadn't expected it?
What changed in you because of it?

2. **Jacob said, "Surely the Lord is in this place, and I did not know it."**
Is there a place in your life now where you're being invited to see holiness where you hadn't before?

3. **What parts of your journey feel uncertain, like Jacob's?**
Where might you need to hear again: *"I am with you. I will watch over you wherever you go"?*

4. **What do you do with your regrets or missteps?**
How does Jacob's story speak to the grace that can meet us even in our failures?

5. **If you were to mark a moment in your life as 'holy ground,' what would it be?**
What made it sacred?

6. **Jacob used a stone (something hard and ordinary) and made it an altar.**
Is there something in your life right now that could become sacred if you looked at it differently?

Jacob Wrestling with the Angel ...

a story of struggle, transformation, and divine encounter.
Genesis 32:22–32

Jacob had been on the road for many years, but there was something he could not outrun: his past, his deceit, and his strained relationship with his brother Esau. After years of separation, they were about to meet again, and Jacob feared what might happen. Would Esau forgive him, or would he seek revenge?

That night, as Jacob crossed the Jabbok River, he found himself alone. And then something strange happened. A man, or perhaps an angel, appeared and began to wrestle with him. They struggled through the night, neither one giving up. Jacob held on with all his strength, refusing to let go.

As dawn broke, the man touched Jacob's hip, dislocating it. But Jacob would not release him. Instead, he clung to the stranger and demanded a blessing.

The man asked, "What is your name?"

"Jacob," he replied.

Then the man said, "Your name will no longer be Jacob, but Israel, because you have struggled with God and with humans and have overcome."

And in that moment, Jacob received a new name and a new identity. He had wrestled with God, and though he was left with a limp, he had been transformed. As he walked away, he named the place *Peniel* —**"Face of God" —**saying, "I have seen God face to face, and yet my life was spared."

Reflection

Jacob's wrestling is symbolic of the human struggle; the tension between who we have been, who we are, and who we are meant to become. Jacob had always lived by his wits, by his own strength, by his ability to deceive. But on this night, he came face to face with something far more powerful than his own will: *God's transformative grace.*

The wrestling match wasn't a contest of strength alone. It was a contest of surrender, of vulnerability, of seeking something deeper than mere survival. Jacob's willingness to hold on through the night, even in pain, was his way of saying, "I want more than just safety. I want blessing. I want transformation."

In the end, Jacob didn't walk away unscathed. His hip was injured, but it was this very wound that marked his transformation. Sometimes, it is the moments of struggle, of being broken and made whole, that lead us to our true calling.

A Sister's Light

"She wasn't afraid of hard questions. She didn't shy away from difficult moments, and that made her a steady companion. She told me her disability after the accident, had happened for a reason. Despite losing her ability to walk, it was something she never resented. She had seen it in a dream and it was as if God/the Divine had helped prepare her for it. She wrestled with God in ways that left her stronger and more whole. Her faith wasn't a shield from pain, but a way to transform it."

Journalling Invitations

1. **When have you had to wrestle with something deep inside yourself, something that would not let go?**
What did that struggle teach you about God, about yourself, or about life?

2. **Jacob's name was changed after his wrestling match.**
Have you ever experienced a moment when your identity or perspective changed (after a struggle or after a breakthrough)?

3. **The wrestling match left Jacob with a limp, but it also gave him a new blessing.**
Is there something in your life that has left you wounded, but also more whole?

4. **What would it look like to wrestle with God in your own life; not as a fight to win, but as a desire for blessing and transformation?**

Bible Stories for the Reflective Heart

5. Jacob demanded a blessing before he would release his hold.

What blessings are you holding onto, or hoping for, in the midst of a struggle?

6. How does the story of Jacob's struggle speak to your own path of faith?

Do you feel that struggle is part of your spiritual journey? Why or why not?

Joseph's Dreams and His Journey to Egypt

Genesis 37:1–36; 39:1–23; 41:1–46

Joseph, the favoured son of Jacob, was marked by his father's special love, which made his eleven brothers bitter with envy. When Joseph shared his dreams (dreams in which his family bowed down to him) his brothers' resentment deepened.

In one of the most painful moments of his life, Joseph's brothers, driven by jealousy, sold him into slavery. They deceived their father, telling him that Joseph had been killed by a wild animal, and Jacob mourned deeply for his son.

Joseph was taken to Egypt, where he was sold to Potiphar, an officer of Pharaoh. There, despite his circumstances, Joseph found favour with his master and was put in charge of Potiphar's household. But when Potiphar's wife falsely accused him of wrongdoing, Joseph was thrown into prison.

Even in prison, Joseph's integrity and wisdom stood out. He interpreted the dreams of Pharaoh's cupbearer and baker, and later, when Pharaoh himself had troubling dreams, the cupbearer remembered Joseph. Joseph was summoned and he interpreted Pharaoh's dreams, foretelling seven years of plenty followed by seven years of famine. Impressed by his wisdom, Pharaoh appointed Joseph as second-in-command over all of Egypt.

The famine that Joseph had predicted struck the land, and here we return to Jacob, Joseph's father, who sent his sons to Egypt to buy grain. When they came before Joseph, they did not recognise him. After testing their character, Joseph revealed his identity to them, and in a moment of great emotion, he forgave them. He invited his father and family to come and live in Egypt, where they would be provided for during the years of famine.

Joseph's dreams had come true, but not in the way anyone had expected. Through suffering, betrayal, and years of waiting, God had worked out a plan of salvation; not only for Joseph but for the entire family of Israel.

Reflection

Joseph's story is one of transformation. It began with the naive dreams of a young man, surrounded by envy and betrayal. Yet, through every trial — being sold into slavery, falsely accused, thrown into prison — Joseph's faith remained. He didn't understand why things were happening the way they were, but he continued to trust that God was with him, even in the darkest moments.

Joseph teaches us about **the unseen hand of providence**. Though he experienced great suffering, he also grew in wisdom and integrity. When the time was right, everything he had endured was used for a greater purpose: not only to save his family, but to set in motion God's larger plan of redemption for Israel.

Joseph's ability to forgive his brothers, despite their treachery, reflects the depth of his transformation. The God who had spoken to him through dreams as a boy had shaped him into a man who could act with mercy, humility, and wisdom.

Dreams have always held a special place in my family's spiritual lives; whether they're seen as messages, visions, or moments of clarity that guide us on our paths.

In Joseph's story, his dreams began as a promise, but it took many years (and many challenges) before they fully came to pass. His dreams spoke to his destiny, but they also became a means of understanding God's purpose in moments of struggle and waiting.

My own belief in the power of dreams echoes that same sense of **divine connection,** that dreams can hold meaning, offering glimpses of understanding or guidance that we might not receive in our waking hours. Sometimes, like Joseph, we may not fully understand the message at first, but it can reveal itself over time, through patience and faith.

And just as I feel dreams can be a source of guidance, Joseph's story reminds us that **the meaning of a dream**

may not be immediate, but over time, its significance will unfold, bringing clarity and understanding.

Like Joseph, Maureen and I have always believed that dreams can carry deep messages, guiding us through life's challenges. (We wrote a book together about this... happy memories). Sometimes, dreams are whispers of encouragement, other times, glimpses of our future path. May we, like Joseph, trust that even in the darkest moments, God can speak to us through the quiet language of dreams.

A Quote inspired by my Sister's Heart

"She had a way of enduring; of walking through trials and remaining unchanged at her core. It was as though each difficulty made her stronger, deeper wiser. She had a quiet strength that you couldn't help but admire. Her faith wasn't loud, but it was steady."

Journalling Invitations

1. **Joseph's brothers betrayed him out of jealousy.**
   Have you ever experienced betrayal or disappointment from someone close? How did you respond, and what did it teach you about forgiveness?
2. **Joseph endured years of hardship without knowing the ultimate purpose.**
   Are there areas in your life where you feel you're in a season of waiting or suffering?
   How might these experiences be helping to shape your personality?
3. **Joseph's dreams were fulfilled, but not in the way he expected.**
   How have your own dreams unfolded in unexpected ways?
   How did this surprise you?

4. **Joseph forgave his brothers, saying, "You intended to harm me, but God intended it for good."**

Is there an area in your life where you can see God redeeming something meant for harm?

What good has come from difficult circumstances?

5. **Joseph rose from a slave to second-in-command in Egypt.**

What qualities in Joseph allowed him to be promoted in the midst of his suffering?

How can you cultivate those qualities in your own life?

6. **Joseph trusted God through years of suffering.**

What does trusting God through hardship look like for you?

How does this story challenge or encourage you to trust more deeply?

We will move on now to the stories of Moses, a central figure in the Bible. Moses was chosen by God to lead the Israelites out of slavery in Egypt and deliver the Ten Commandments, shaping the foundation of faith and law for generations to come.

☽⁺⁺ *Handwritten Reflections* ⁺⁺☽

You are invited to sit quietly with what you've read. Below is space for your own thoughts, prayers, or dreams that rise as you ponder these bible stories and their meaning in your life.

✎ _____

✎ _____

✎ _____

✎ _____

✎ _____

✎ _____

✎ _____

✦ *"The heavens declare the glory of God; the skies proclaim the work of His hands."* — Psalm 19:1 ✦
Let these pages be your sacred sky.

Moses: Drawn from the Water
Exodus 1:22 – 2:10

The Hebrews groaned under Pharaoh's rule, their cries rising like incense to heaven. Fearing their growing numbers, Pharaoh issued a dreadful decree: all Hebrew baby boys must be cast into the Nile.

In this time of fear, a woman from the tribe of Levi bore a son. She saw that he was beautiful, a child full of promise. She hid him for three months, cradling him in whispered lullabies and trembling prayers. When she could no longer conceal him, she crafted a small ark of reeds, sealing it with tar. With careful hands and a breaking heart, she placed him among the reeds of the riverbank, entrusting him to the waters and to God.

His sister, Miriam, watched as the current rocked the little vessel. Then, the unexpected happened: Pharaoh's own daughter came to bathe. She saw the basket, opened it, and the baby's cries stirred compassion in her heart.

"This is one of the Hebrews' children," she murmured.

Miriam stepped forward, courage blooming in her. "Shall I find a nurse for the child?"

Pharaoh's daughter agreed, and so the baby's own mother was chosen to care for him. When he grew older, he was brought into the palace and named Moses, meaning *Drawn Out* — for he was drawn from the water and set apart for a great purpose.

Reflection
Moses' early life is one of divine providence. The very river meant to destroy him became the place of his salvation. His mother's courage, Miriam's watchful heart, and Pharaoh's daughter's unexpected mercy wove together a story of deliverance.

Like Moses, we are sometimes placed in situations that seem overwhelming, where the waters of life feel deep and uncertain. Yet, even in uncertainty, God's hand moves. Moses was cradled by the currents, but he was never abandoned. He was drawn out, protected, and prepared for his calling.

Have there been times in your life when you felt set adrift, unsure of what would come next? Perhaps, like Moses in the reeds, you were being carried toward a destiny greater than you imagined. Sometimes, our salvation comes in ways we do not expect, through people we never anticipated.

Inspired Thought
"The river of fear may surround us, but God always has a plan to draw us out."

Journaling Invitations
1. Recall a time in your life when you felt uncertain or vulnerable. How did God provide for you in unexpected ways?

2. Moses' mother had to let go of him, trusting God with his future. Is there something in your life you need to release into God's hands?

3. Reflect on a time when someone showed you unexpected kindness or mercy. How did that moment shape your journey?

4. Imagine you are Miriam, watching over Moses. Who in your life needs your watchful care and support right now?

May you find peace in knowing that even when the waters seem deep, there is always a hand reaching to draw you out.

Moses and the Burning Bush

Exodus 3:1–12

Moses had fled Egypt years ago, a prince turned shepherd, hiding from the memory of his past. He had once been part of Pharaoh's court, but after killing an Egyptian who was mistreating a Hebrew slave, Moses ran for his life. For forty years, he tended sheep in the wilderness, far from the people of Egypt, far from his calling.

One day, as he tended the flock on Mount Horeb, he saw something strange: a bush that was on fire, but not consumed by the flames. As he approached, a voice called his name from the bush.

"Moses! Moses!"

"Here I am," he answered.

"Do not come any closer. Take off your sandals, for the place where you are standing is holy ground."

Then God spoke, revealing His identity: **"I am the God of your father, the God of Abraham, the God of Isaac, and the God of Jacob."**

Moses hid his face in fear.

But God continued, revealing His plan: **"I have seen the misery of My people in Egypt. I have heard their cries. I am sending you to Pharaoh to bring My people out of Egypt."**

Moses, filled with doubt, questioned God: *"Who am I to go to Pharaoh? How can I lead the Israelites out of Egypt?"*

But God reassured him: **"I will be with you. This will be a sign to you that I am sending you: When you have brought the people out of Egypt, you will worship God on this mountain."**

Moses wasn't convinced. He needed more reassurance, but God's call remained firm. He would be the one to lead the Israelites to freedom.

Reflection

This moment was the intersection of **Moses' past, present, and future**. For years, he had lived in exile, far from the people he once identified with. Now, God was calling him back to a place of pain and unresolved conflict to confront

Pharaoh, the very one who had sent him running. It was a call that Moses resisted, but it was also a call of divine purpose.

The burning bush was a **sign of God's presence**, and it spoke not only of the divine call but also of the holy ground Moses was standing on. It reminds us that we too may encounter God in the most unlikely of places, in moments of uncertainty, and even in the places where we have struggled. Moses' hesitation reminds us of our own fears and doubts when we are called to step out of our comfort zone, but God's answer is always clear: **"I will be with you."**

Moses didn't have to be perfect or confident. He just had to be willing. And when he was, God provided everything he needed. Just like Moses, Christians believe that we are often called not because of our own strength, but because of God's strength working through us.

From a neutral perspective:

Moses stands before the burning bush, a man caught between past and future, between identity and duty. The flame burns but does not consume, much like the callings that stir within us, persistent, illuminating, yet never destroying.

This moment is one of transformation. Moses is no longer just a shepherd; he is confronted with a truth larger than himself. How often do we, too, hesitate when faced with something that demands more of us? We question our worthiness, our ability, our readiness. But the voice from the fire does not ask for perfection; it simply calls.

The burning bush also represents a paradox: fire that does not destroy, a leader who begins with reluctance, power that is found in humility. Life is full of these contradictions, and wisdom often lies in holding space for them rather than resolving them.

What fires burn in your life, calling you to something greater? Do you resist, or do you listen? And if you were to step forward, what might you become?

A Sister's Light

"She always knew when something was calling her to move forward, even when it was difficult. She could be still and listen for the voice of God in her life, and when she heard it, she responded with courage, even if she felt afraid. She knew the difference between fear and purpose, and always chose purpose."

Journalling Invitations

1. **Moses heard God's call from the burning bush, a place he never expected to be holy.**
Have you ever experienced a moment where something unexpected or ordinary became holy?
What made it so?

2. **Moses questioned God's choice, asking, "Who am I to do this?"**
Have you ever felt unworthy or unprepared for something God has called you to do?
How did you respond to that feeling?

3. **God reassured Moses, saying, "I will be with you."**
When have you needed God's reassurance in your own life?
How did it change your approach to the challenges you faced?

4. **Moses had to confront his past to fulfil his calling.**
Are there areas of your past that you are avoiding, but which God is calling you to face?
What steps might you take to confront them with faith?

5. **God didn't give Moses all the answers at once; He simply gave him the next step.**
How do you handle uncertainty or lack of clarity in your own journey?
What does it look like to trust God for the next step?

6. The place where Moses stood was holy ground.

Are there places in your life that could be transformed into holy ground by recognising God's presence?

How can you treat these moments with reverence and awareness?

This last question suggests that *any* moment, place, or experience (however ordinary, painful, or overlooked) can become holy when we become aware that God is present in it.

It might be:

- A place of sorrow, where you felt abandoned or misunderstood.
- A daily task that feels mundane or exhausting.
- A difficult memory you avoid revisiting.
- A waiting season, a crossroads, or even a hospital room. Recognising God's presence in these places can change how we see them. They become not just scenes of hardship or routine, but sacred spaces where God met us, sustained us, or quietly worked behind the veil.

Moses and the Plagues in Egypt

Exodus 7:14–12:30

Moses, now fully embracing his role as God's chosen leader, stood before Pharaoh with a message that was as difficult as it was urgent: "Let my people go." But Pharaoh's heart was hardened, and he refused to listen. The stage was set for a divine showdown between God and the ruler of Egypt.

God sent ten plagues upon Egypt to convince Pharaoh to let the Israelites go. Each plague was a demonstration of God's power and judgement, targeting Egypt's gods and the pride of Pharaoh himself.

1. **The Nile turned to blood** — the very river that sustained Egypt became a source of death and misery.

2. **Frogs overran the land**, covering everything, making life unbearable.

3. **Gnats filled the air**, a swarm so great it could not be escaped.

4. **Flies invaded homes** and fields, further escalating the chaos.

5. **The livestock died**, leaving Egypt's economy in ruins.

6. **Boils appeared on the people and animals**, painful and unrelenting.

7. **Hail and fire rained down**, destroying crops and fields.

8. **Locusts devoured what remained**, leaving nothing in their wake.

9. **Darkness covered the land** for three days, a thick, oppressive darkness that could be felt.

10. **The final plague** struck — **the death of the firstborn**. This last plague would break Pharaoh's resolve and lead to the Israelites' exodus from Egypt.

The **death of the firstborn** was the most devastating of all, and it marked a pivotal moment in the story. God had instructed Moses to prepare the Israelites for the final and most devastating plague in Egypt — the death of every firstborn. But God also gave His people a way to be spared.

Each Israelite household was to take a lamb without blemish and, on the appointed night, **sacrifice the lamb**. They were to take **some of its blood** and mark it on the **doorposts and lintel** — the sides and top of the doorway. Then they were to remain inside their homes and share a sacred meal of roasted lamb, bitter herbs, and unleavened bread.

That night, the **angel of death passed through Egypt**, bringing judgement. But wherever the angel saw the lamb's blood on the door, it **passed over** that home, sparing the firstborn within.

This moment became known as the **Passover**, a lasting sign of God's deliverance. The blood marked God's protection; not because of the people's perfection, but because of their trust and obedience.

The plague led to Pharaoh finally releasing the Israelites, who began their journey to freedom.

Reflection

The plagues demonstrate God's power over the forces of nature and the gods of Egypt. They were not random acts of destruction, but intentional signs, each one revealing a facet of God's sovereignty and the consequences of Pharaoh's stubbornness. The story, some believe, reveals a God who is just, patient, and ultimately merciful, even in the midst of judgement.

What stands out in the story is the way Pharaoh's heart became progressively harder, even in the face of undeniable signs of divine power. God's patience was tested, and yet each plague brought Pharaoh closer to the moment of release. **God was working even through Pharaoh's resistance**, bringing about His purpose despite the resistance of those in power.

For the Israelites, the plagues were not just acts of judgement on Egypt; they were acts of **deliverance**: God moving to rescue them, to fulfil the promises made to their ancestors. The Passover became the sign of God's saving grace, a reminder of His protection and His covenant with His people.

A Reflection on Transformation

The story of Moses and the plagues is often seen as a tale of divine power, but at its heart, it is also a story of transformation. The plagues were not just external calamities, they mirrored the inner resistance of Pharaoh, the hardened heart that refused change.

In life, we often cling to what is familiar, even when it no longer serves us. We resist growth, fearing what lies beyond the comfort of our known world. But just as the plagues escalated until Pharaoh had no choice but to let go, life, too, sends us signals (small nudges at first, then louder calls) urging us to release what binds us and step into a greater freedom.

The journey of Moses reminds us that liberation is not easy. It demands courage, trust, and the willingness to walk through uncertainty. Yet, on the other side of struggle, there is transformation. The plagues, then, are not just about destruction; they are about breaking through resistance so that something new can emerge.

Where in our own lives do we resist change? What signs (subtle or severe) is life offering us to move forward? If we listen, perhaps we, too, can find our path to freedom.

A Sister's Light

"She understood what it meant to wait, to endure through seasons of hardship. Even when things didn't seem to change, she believed that God/the Divine was still at work. Like the plagues, she knew that sometimes change comes slowly, but she always trusted in divine timing."

Journalling Invitations

1. **Pharaoh's heart was hardened, and he refused to listen to the signs God sent.**
Have you ever found yourself resistant to something God was trying to teach you?
How did you finally open your heart to His message?

2. **The plagues were not just acts of destruction, but acts of deliverance for Israel.**
In your life, have you ever seen something difficult turn into something that led to freedom or deliverance?
What was that experience like?

3. **The Israelites were spared during the final plague through the blood of the lamb.**
How does the story of the Passover remind you of God's saving grace?
In what areas of your life have you experienced God's protection or mercy?

4. **Pharaoh's refusal to listen to God led to great suffering.**
Have you ever seen the consequences of ignoring or resisting God's call in your own life, or in the lives of others?
What can you learn from that?

5. **What Disrupts also reveals:** The plagues brought disruption—sudden, jarring, undeniable. Life changed overnight, again and again. They forced people to stop, to reckon, to see what had been hidden in plain sight.
Have you ever gone through a season of disruption —a time when everything you knew was turned upside down? - What did that time *reveal* to you about yourself, others, or the systems you lived within?

6. Have there been truths you couldn't ignore any longer? What emerged in the stillness after the chaos?

The Parting of the Red Sea

Exodus 14:1–31

The Israelites had finally been set free, but their journey out of Egypt wasn't without its own challenges. Pharaoh, after letting them go, had a change of heart and pursued them with his army, intent on bringing them back into captivity. The Israelites, now trapped between Pharaoh's army and the Red Sea, were faced with a seemingly impossible situation.

Moses cried out to God, and God responded by telling him to raise his staff over the sea. Then the Lord said to Moses, *'Why are you crying out to Me? Tell the Israelites to move on. Raise your staff and stretch out your hand over the sea to divide the water so that the Israelites can go through the sea on dry ground.'"*

As Moses did this, a powerful wind blew all night, parting the waters and creating a path of dry ground through the sea. The Israelites walked through the sea with walls of water on their right and left.

Pharaoh's army, in pursuit of the Israelites, followed them into the sea. But just as the last of the Israelites had crossed, God instructed Moses to stretch his hand back over the sea. As Moses did, the waters returned to their original place, drowning Pharaoh's chariots and soldiers.

The Israelites were safe on the other side, and they **celebrated** with songs of praise to God, rejoicing in His great power and deliverance.

Reflection

The crossing of the Red Sea was not just a physical act of salvation for the Israelites, but a moment of deep faith and obedience. In the face of the overwhelming obstacle of the sea, they were called to step forward, trusting that God would make a way where there seemed to be none.

Moses' trust in God's promise was key in this moment. He didn't know how God would part the sea, but he obeyed the command to raise his staff in faith. **God's intervention** came after obedience, showing that sometimes we are called to move forward in faith, even when the way is unclear.

The imagery of walking through the sea, with walls of water towering on either side, reminds us that sometimes we must move through difficult circumstances in order to reach the freedom God has promised. It is not without fear, not without uncertainty, but it is with trust that God/the Divine will **make a way**.

And when we reach the other side, like the Israelites, there is **praise and worship**, a deep recognition that it is only by God's power/the power of the Divine that we were able to make it through.

From a neutral perspective:

The parting of the Red Sea is often seen as a moment of divine intervention, a miraculous escape from danger. But beyond its religious significance, it carries a universal message about trust, transformation, and the unknown.

At its heart, the story speaks of that moment when we stand at the edge of our own fears, with no clear path forward. Behind us, the past presses in (old patterns, doubts, and struggles), while ahead lies only uncertainty. Like those at the water's edge, we often hesitate, waiting for a sign that it's safe to step forward.

Yet the sea does not part until the first step is taken. The way through is not revealed until we move in faith ... not necessarily faith in a higher power, but faith in ourselves, in the unfolding of life, in the unseen forces that guide us toward growth.

Transformation is rarely comfortable. The crossing of the sea was not a leisurely walk; it was likely filled with fear and disbelief. But to move forward, we must be willing to pass through that space of uncertainty, trusting that solid ground will appear beneath our feet.

Perhaps the Red Sea reminds us that the obstacles before us are not always barriers, but thresholds. When we find the courage to step into the unknown, what once seemed impossible begins to open before us. The waters do not part first, we walk first, and then the way is made clear.

A Quote inspired by my sister's Spirit

"She always knew that God would make a way, even when it seemed impossible. When faced with difficulties, she moved forward in faith, knowing that the obstacles would give way to something greater. Her trust in God/the Divine was unwavering, even when the path wasn't clear."

Journalling Invitations

1. **The Israelites faced an impossible situation at the Red Sea, but they obeyed and trusted God.**
What are some obstacles you have faced that seemed insurmountable?
How did you respond? How did God make a way for you?

2. **Moses raised his staff in faith, even before seeing how God would part the sea.**
Are there areas in your life where God/your intuition is asking you to take a step of faith before you see the full picture?

3. **The Israelites had to move through the sea, surrounded by walls of water.**
What does it mean to move through difficult circumstances, trusting that God is with you?
How can you lean into God's presence during trials?

4. **When they reached the other side, the Israelites sang songs of praise to God.**
How do you celebrate God's deliverance in your life?
When you have experienced a breakthrough or answered prayer, how do you express your gratitude?

5. **The Israelites had to leave behind Egypt, a place of bondage, to find freedom in the wilderness.**
Is there anything in your life that God is calling you to

leave behind in order to experience freedom?
What steps can you take to move forward?

6. **The Red Sea parting was a moment of God's power and intervention.**

Are there moments in your life when you've witnessed God's miraculous intervention?

How can you hold on to these moments to strengthen your faith during times of uncertainty?

Let's continue with the journey of the Israelites through the wilderness, a time of both testing and strengthening spiritual growth. While the Israelites had been freed from Egypt, their journey toward the Promised Land was not immediate or easy. God's provision, guidance, and lessons for His people are revealed in some of their most challenging moments.

The Journey through the Wilderness

Exodus 16–17, Numbers 11

After the miraculous crossing of the Red Sea, the Israelites began their journey through the wilderness, a journey that would last forty years. The path was not straight; it was full of challenges, tests, and opportunities to deepen their trust in God.

The Manna and Quail

As the Israelites travelled, they began to grumble. They were hungry and thirsty, longing for the food they had in Egypt, despite their slavery. They complained to Moses, saying, *"If only we had died by the Lord's hand in Egypt! There we sat around pots of meat and ate all the food we wanted, but you have brought us out into this desert to starve this entire assembly to death."*

In response, God provided manna, a bread-like substance that appeared on the ground each morning, and quail, which flew into the camp in the evening. For forty years, God provided this food for the Israelites. "I will rain down bread from heaven for you," God told Moses. The manna was a daily provision that required the people to trust God each day for their needs.

Water from the Rock

In another moment of desperation, the Israelites began to complain again, this time about the lack of water. They quarrelled with Moses, asking, *"Why did you bring us up out of Egypt to make us and our children and livestock die of thirst?"* Once again, God responded. He instructed Moses to strike a rock at Horeb, and when he did, water poured out for the people to drink.

The Battle with the Amalekites

As they continued their journey, the Israelites were attacked by the Amalekites, a people who sought to defeat them. Moses, with the help of his companions, lifted his hands in prayer, and as long as his hands were raised, the Israelites prevailed. When his hands grew tired, the Amalekites gained ground. So,

Aaron and Hur supported Moses, holding his hands up until the victory was won.

Reflection

The wilderness was a place of testing and transformation. It was where the Israelites learned to rely completely on God. The challenges they faced (hunger, thirst, and attacks) were opportunities for them to deepen their trust in God's provision, power, and protection. God used these difficult times to shape their character, teaching them that He was not just the God who parted the Red Sea, but the God who would provide their daily bread and sustain them in every circumstance.

Their complaints and grumbling were signs of their lack of trust in God's provision. They wanted the comfort of Egypt, forgetting that slavery, no matter how familiar, was never truly a place of peace. God, in His mercy, provided for them time and time again, but each provision was an invitation to trust Him more fully.

In the wilderness, God's faithfulness was evident. The manna and quail were a tangible sign of His care, the water from the rock a reminder that He would meet their needs, and the victory over the Amalekites a demonstration of His strength. But it also required obedience: listening to God, trusting His directions, and remaining faithful to the path He had set.

From a neutral perspective:

The journey through the wilderness is a story of transformation; a passage from what was, through the unknown, to what will be. It is the space between leaving behind an old life and stepping into a new one, a space of uncertainty, challenge, and discovery.

In many ways, we all experience our own wilderness. It is the time after loss, when the familiar is gone but the future has not yet taken shape. It is the space of change: between one job and the next, one home and another, one version of ourselves and the person we are becoming. The wilderness is uncomfortable, but it is also where we learn resilience.

There are no shortcuts through this kind of journey. It cannot be rushed, nor can we skip ahead to the destination. The wilderness forces us to be present, to listen, to trust in the unfolding of life even when the path is unclear. It teaches patience, surrender, and self-reliance.

Yet, the wilderness is not only a place of hardship; it is also a place of deep transformation. When everything familiar falls away, we discover what truly sustains us. We learn to let go of what no longer serves us, to rely on inner strength, and to recognise the quiet wisdom that can only be heard in stillness.

Emerging from the wilderness, we are never quite the same. We carry with us the lessons of perseverance, the knowledge that we can navigate the unknown, and the quiet assurance that even in life's most uncertain moments, we are always on our way to something new.

A Sister's Light

"She always found a way to see the Divine at work in the ordinary moments, even in the wilderness seasons of life. It was in those moments of discomfort, when the path seemed unclear, that she experienced the Divine in the most surprising ways. She knew that God/the Divine would provide, even if the journey wasn't easy."

Journalling Invitations

1. **The Israelites complained about their hunger and thirst.**
Have you ever found yourself questioning God's provision in difficult times?
How did He provide for you, even when you couldn't see a way forward?

2. **God provided manna each day, a daily provision.**
What daily provisions are you grateful for?
How can you cultivate trust in God's faithfulness for your daily needs?

3. **Moses struck the rock to bring forth water.**

Are there "rocks" in your life that feel hard or barren, yet God wants to bring forth blessings from them?

How can you trust God to provide in unexpected ways?

4. **The Israelites were tested and sometimes failed to trust God fully.**

Have there been moments in your life when you struggled to trust God's plan?

What have you learned from those moments?

5. **Moses raised his hands in prayer during the battle with the Amalekites.**

How do you raise your "hands" in prayer when facing challenges?

How does prayer strengthen your faith in moments of spiritual battle?

6. **The wilderness was a place of both testing and transformation.**

How has God transformed you during your own "wilderness" seasons?

How can you continue to grow in trust during times of uncertainty or trial?

Let's continue with the **giving of the Ten Commandments,** one of the most foundational moments in the journey of the Israelites. This moment marks a deepening of the covenant between God and His people, a call to holiness, and a set of guidelines for living in relationship with God and one another.

The Ten Commandments

Exodus 19:16–20:21

The Israelites, after their miraculous deliverance and journey through the wilderness, arrived at Mount Sinai, where God called Moses up to the mountain to receive the law. For three days, the people prepared themselves, knowing that something extraordinary was about to take place. They washed their clothes and consecrated themselves in anticipation of encountering God.

On the third day, thunder and lightning surrounded the mountain, and a thick cloud covered it. The people could hear the sound of a trumpet blast, growing louder and louder. The mountain itself was trembling, as if it was alive. It was in this awe-inspiring and fear-inducing moment that God called Moses to the top of the mountain.

God spoke to Moses, giving him the Ten Commandments, which would serve as the foundation of Israel's covenant with God and the guiding principles for their lives. The commandments were clear and direct, covering all aspects of life, from how to worship God to how to treat one another.

Here are the Ten Commandments, as given in **Exodus 20:1-17**:

1. **You shall have no other gods before Me.**
The Israelites were to worship God alone and to place no other gods before Him.

2. **You shall not make for yourselves a carved image.**
God forbids the creation of idols, reminding the people that He is a jealous God.

3. **You shall not take the name of the Lord your God in vain.**
Respect for God's name and holiness is to be upheld in speech and action.

4. **Remember the Sabbath day, to keep it holy.**

A day of rest and worship is set aside for renewal and honouring God.

    5. **Honour your father and your mother.**
Respect for parents is foundational for a well-ordered society.

    6. **You shall not murder.**
God calls His people to value life and to live in peace with others.

    7. **You shall not commit adultery.**
Faithfulness in marriage is essential for healthy relationships and communities.

    8. **You shall not steal.**
Respect for others' property and rights is commanded.

    9. **You shall not bear false witness against your neighbour.**
Truthfulness is a core value in relationships and society.

    10. **You shall not covet.**
Contentment with what one has and respect for others' possessions is emphasised.

After God gave Moses the commandments, the Israelites were afraid to come near the mountain, overwhelmed by the visible manifestation of God's presence. Moses, acting as the mediator between God and the people, received further instructions from God on how they were to live in obedience to His law.

Reflection on the Ten Commandments

The Ten Commandments were not just rules; they were a revelation of God's character and a blueprint for how to have a good relationship with Him and others. They marked the Israelites as a holy people, set apart to reflect God's nature in the world.

The first four commandments speak of our relationship with God: how we are to honour Him, worship Him alone, and keep His name sacred. These commandments serve as a foundation for all the others, as love for God becomes the driving force behind all our actions.

The remaining six commandments focus on **how we live with one another**: how we treat our parents, our neighbours, and our communities. These commandments emphasise the sanctity of life, the importance of honesty, the value of fidelity in relationships, and the need for contentment.

In giving these commandments, God was not only providing the Israelites with guidelines for living, but He was also calling them into a deeper, more intimate relationship with Himself. The commandments were a **gift**; a way for the Israelites to experience the blessings of living in obedience to God, and a way for them to share with surrounding nations what it meant to be a people who followed God.

Additional Thoughts

Reflection on the First Commandment: "You shall have no other gods before Me."

This commandment, at its heart, calls people into an undivided relationship with the Divine. It is not merely a rule but an invitation: to place what is eternal above what is fleeting; to centre our lives on what truly matters.

In a world full of distractions, it is easy to let other "gods" take root: ambition, approval, possessions, even fear. These are not golden idols but subtle attachments that pull our attention away from the sacred/divine.

To honour this commandment is to live with clarity of heart. It is to say, "I choose what is true. I choose what is eternal. I choose to root myself in love, in trust, in the mystery of God/the universe."

It is not about exclusion, but devotion: a realignment of soul to the One who gives life meaning and breath.

In this way, the first commandment becomes a compass, gently guiding us home.

Reflection on the Second Commandment: "You shall not make for yourselves a carved image."

This commandment is not only about graven statues; it speaks of the deeper human tendency to limit the infinite.

When we try to capture God in a fixed form, whether in stone, idea, or even personal certainty, we risk shrinking the mystery into something we can control.

The sacred cannot be carved, contained, or confined. It moves beyond what the eye can see and the hand can shape. True reverence requires humility; the kind that allows for wonder, for silence, for awe.

To live this commandment is to remember that God is not a possession, not an object of our making, but the source of all being. It is an invitation to release our need for certainty and to step into the spaciousness of faith, where love, not image, reveals the Divine.

The phrase *"for I am a jealous God"* can feel unsettling at first. Jealousy is not a trait we often associate with the Divine. But in the context of the Ten Commandments, it speaks not of petty envy, but of passionate, covenantal love. God's "jealousy" reflects a deep desire for faithfulness, much like that of a loving spouse who longs for an undivided heart.

This is not a possessive demand, but an invitation into a relationship of exclusive devotion—where God, for Christians, is not one of many, but the One and only. Just as love between people is diminished by divided loyalty, so too is our relationship with God harmed when we place our trust in lesser things.

God's jealousy is a reminder of how fiercely we are loved. Not out of control, but full of purpose. God is not distant or indifferent—He cares deeply, and calls us to love Him in return with our whole hearts.

From a non-religious perspective, the phrase *"for I am a jealous God"* can be seen as a symbolic expression of the human need for loyalty, presence, and meaning. In this light, "God" may represent not a deity, but our highest values (truth, love, integrity, or purpose). The "jealousy" here is not possessiveness, but a metaphor for how our deeper commitments call us back when we stray.

We all have inner compasses: core values that demand our attention. When we divide our loyalty, perhaps chasing success at the cost of integrity, or comfort over courage, something within us stirs. This "jealous" voice is not angry, but firm, asking, *"Remember who you are. Remember what really matters."*

It's a reminder that devotion to what is most meaningful in life is not passive. It asks something of us. It wants our focus, our action, and our faithfulness, even when other paths seem easier.

Reflection on the Fourth Commandment: "Remember the Sabbath day, to keep it holy."

In a world that glorifies busyness, the Sabbath offers a quiet rebellion; a sacred pause in the rhythm of life. To remember the Sabbath is to remember our own humanity, our need for rest, for breath, for being rather than doing.

This commandment is not just about a day; it is about a way of seeing. It calls us to honour the holy in time itself, to step outside the noise and into stillness.

Keeping the Sabbath holy is an act of trust ... trust that the world can turn without our constant striving, and that our worth is not measured by productivity, but by presence.

In this rest, we return to ourselves. And in that return, we remember God/the Divine.

Reflection on the Fifth Commandment: Honour your father and your mother.

To honour father and mother is to recognise the roots from which we come: the lives, choices, and sacrifices that shaped our beginning. It is a commandment that invites gratitude, not only for the gift of life, but for the threads of love, imperfection, and legacy woven into our story.

Honouring does not mean blind obedience, nor does it ignore pain or complexity. It means holding our parents—and our past—with compassion and respect, even as we grow into being our own person.

This commandment reaches beyond family; it refers to a deeper reverence for all who came before us. To honour is to remember we are part of something larger: a lineage, a history, a sacred continuity of life.

Further thoughts: This commandment is often interpreted as a call to respect, value, and care for one's parents, acknowledging the life and guidance they have given. But what if a parent has been abusive — emotionally, physically, or spiritually? In this instance, this verse can be painful or confusing. How can one "honour" a person who caused harm?

Remember that honouring does not mean putting yourself in harm's way, tolerating abuse, or pretending that wrongs didn't happen. God does not expect us to be passive in the face of injustice or to overlook what is sinful.

Many people have experienced difficult childhoods, enduring emotional, physical, or mental hardships as a result of their upbringing and parental circumstances/treatment of them.

To honour a parent may mean acknowledging the truth of what happened, while choosing not to continue in the same vein. This may necessitate setting healthy boundaries, refusing to lie about the past, but also refusing to be consumed by hatred.

Honouring can be choosing compassion over vengeance. This might include praying for them, even if contact isn't safe or possible. It might mean handing judgement over to God/the Divine/your Angels, trusting Him/Them with the pain and choosing not to let bitterness take root.

This commandment can be seen not only as a call to show respect but also as an invitation to live with integrity; reflecting the values of love, dignity, and healing that may not have been modelled to you. In this way, you honour the *role* of parenthood, even if the person did not fulfil it well.

Sometimes the greatest act of honour is to live a life of love, strength, and faithfulness in spite of what was experienced in childhood — to break the cycle. To become the kind of person you needed them to be.

If you're working through this personally, it is fine to take your time. Healing is sacred work. God knows your heart, your story, and your pain. He is not asking for blind obedience, but for a spirit of truth and grace.

Reflection on the Sixth Commandment: "You shall not murder."

At its core, this commandment affirms the sacredness of life. It reminds us that each human being carries within them the breath of the Divine: a mystery too precious to be extinguished by violence.

To not murder is more than a prohibition against physical harm; it is a call to live with reverence for the lives of others. It invites us to examine the quieter ways we may diminish life ... through hatred, cruelty, or indifference.

This commandment draws a line: life is not ours to take. It teaches restraint, yes, but also responsibility: to protect, to preserve, and to choose compassion over harm.

In honouring life, we honour the Creator who gave it.

Reflection on the Seventh Commandment: "You shall not commit adultery."

This commandment highlights the sacredness of trust: the quiet covenant that binds hearts together in love and fidelity. To commit adultery is not only to break a promise, but to wound the deeper fabric of relationship where vulnerability and truth are meant to dwell.

It reminds us that love is not merely a feeling, but a commitment tended with honesty, respect, and care. When we honour that commitment, we reflect something of the Divine faithfulness that never betrays or forgets.

In a world of shifting loyalties, this commandment stands as a call to integrity: to love with wholeness, and to let our promises be a reflection of the steadfast love we all long to receive.

Reflection on the Eighth Commandment: "You shall not steal."

At its heart, this commandment speaks of the dignity of others and the integrity of our actions. Stealing is not merely the taking of possessions; it is a violation of trust and a disregard for the rights of others. It disrupts the balance of respect and fairness that sustains human relationships.

To honour this commandment is to recognise that all that we have (our resources, our time, our very lives) are gifts. To take what does not belong to us is to disrupt the flow of generosity and justice that connects us all.

In living with honesty, we affirm that each person's right to their own is sacred, and that true wealth is found not in what we possess, but in how we honour the worth of others.

Reflection on the Ninth Commandment: "You shall not bear false witness against your neighbour."

This commandment reminds us of the truth, not just in words, but in the integrity of our actions and intentions. Bearing false witness is not simply telling lies; it is the distortion of reality, the twisting of facts to harm or deceive. In doing so, we damage not only others, but ourselves, for dishonesty fractures the trust that binds humanity together.

To honour this commandment is to value truth, not as an abstract concept, but as a living, breathing force that nurtures relationships, justice, and peace. It reminds us that our words have power to create or destroy, and that to speak truthfully is to uphold the dignity of all.

In a world where the line between truth and falsehood can blur, this commandment is a call to clarity: to speak with kindness, humility, and respect, so that our words reflect the light of honesty.

Reflection on the Tenth Commandment: "You shall not covet."

This commandment invites us to look inward, urging us to confront the subtle stirrings of envy that can unsettle our inner peace. Coveting is not merely an outward act but a quiet turmoil of the heart. A longing for what is not ours that distracts us from the abundance of our own lives.

By renouncing envy, we open ourselves to gratitude and contentment. We learn to appreciate the blessings that are already present, fostering a sense of wholeness that transcends material desire. In doing so, we not only honour our own worth but also create space for compassion and generosity toward others.

A Sister's Light

"She was a deeply spiritual soul – open-hearted, intuitive and always seeking deeper meaning in life. While her faith was personal and full of wonder, she held firmly to Christian morals. Kindness, honesty, forgiveness and compassion guided her choices. She didn't just believe in these values ... she lived them, quietly and consistently."

Journalling Invitations

1. **The Ten Commandments begin with a call to honour God above all else.**
In what areas of your life do you struggle to keep God first?
How can you cultivate a deeper relationship with God through worship, prayer, and surrender?

2. **The commandments also emphasise the importance of honouring others.**
What does it mean to show honour and respect to others?

3. **The commandments call for a life of truth, fidelity, and peace.**
How can you practice truthfulness in your relationships?
Are there areas where you need to ask for forgiveness or make amends?

4. **"You shall not covet" is a call to contentment and gratitude.**
What areas of your life do you struggle with coveting or comparison?
How can you develop a deeper sense of contentment and thankfulness?

5. **The Ten Commandments are a guide for living in alignment with God's will.**

In what ways do the commandments shape the way you live and act in your daily life?

6.   **God gave the commandments to shape His people into a reflection of His holiness.** How can you align your heart and actions with God's holiness in your life?

From a non-spiritual perspective, the Ten Commandments can be seen as a foundational code of ethics designed to promote harmony and order in society. They address essential principles such as respecting others' rights, honouring commitments, and maintaining honesty and fairness. These guidelines, regardless of religious belief, reflect timeless values that help communities function peacefully, discouraging harm, fostering trust, and encouraging personal responsibility in our interactions with others.

Let's continue now, with the **golden calf** story, a profound moment in the wilderness journey of the Israelites. This story reveals the danger of impatience and the consequences of turning to idols, but it also shows God's incredible mercy and Moses' intercession for the people.

☽✦ *Handwritten Reflections* ✦☽

You are invited to sit quietly with what you've read. Below is space for your own thoughts, prayers, or dreams that rise as you ponder these bible stories and their meaning in your life.

✎ _____

✎ _____

✎ _____

✎ _____

✎ _____

✎ _____

✎ _____

✎ _____

✹ *"The heavens declare the glory of God; the skies proclaim the work of His hands." — Psalm 19:1* ✹
Let these pages be your sacred sky.

The Golden Calf

Exodus 32:1-35

As the Israelites journeyed through the wilderness, they came to a point where Moses, their leader, went up on Mount Sinai to receive further instructions from God. He stayed on the mountain for forty days and forty nights, during which time the people grew restless and uncertain. They wondered where Moses had gone and why he hadn't returned yet.

In their impatience, they turned to Aaron, Moses' brother, and demanded that he make them gods to lead them, saying, *"As for this fellow Moses who brought us up out of Egypt, we don't know what has happened to him."* Aaron, sadly, agreed to their request. He collected gold from the people and fashioned it into a golden calf, declaring, *"These are your gods, O Israel, who brought you up out of Egypt."*

The people worshiped the golden calf, offering sacrifices and engaging in revelry. When Moses came down from the mountain, he saw the people dancing and celebrating before the idol. His anger burned hot, and he threw down the tablets containing the Ten Commandments, breaking them into pieces.

Moses immediately took action. He destroyed the golden calf, grinding it into powder, scattering it on the water, and making the people drink it. He confronted Aaron, asking why he had led the people into such sin, and then he called for those who were still loyal to God to come to him. The **Levites** rallied to Moses' side, and he instructed them to go through the camp and strike down those who had participated in the idolatry.

That day about three thousand people perished as a result of their sin. (It was also said that a plague was sent upon the people as punishment). Moses then went back to God to plead for the people's forgiveness. He acknowledged the gravity of their sin and asked God to forgive them, even offering his own life as a sacrifice if necessary. But God, in His mercy, allowed the people to live, though He sent a plague upon them as punishment for their actions.

Reflection

The story of the golden calf is an important lesson about impatience and the temptation to turn to idols when we feel abandoned or uncertain. The Israelites had just experienced the miraculous deliverance of God, and yet in a moment of waiting, they quickly turned to a false god in the form of a golden calf. This moment highlights the danger of idolatry, not just in the physical sense, but in the way we often turn to false comforts, desires, or distractions when we feel lost or anxious.

Moses' response shows his devotion to God and his desire to protect the people from the consequences of their sin. His intercession is an example of a leader who stands in the gap for others, pleading for mercy even when the people have made grave mistakes.

At the same time, this story reminds us that sin has consequences. The Israelites' turning to the golden calf resulted in death and punishment, but it also resulted in a deeper understanding of God's holiness and justice. Even though God forgave them, they had to face the consequences of their actions.

And yet, God's mercy shines through. Even when the people fall into sin, God does not abandon them but offers a way to return to Him through repentance. Moses' role as an intercessor points to God's grace, which allows for restoration, even after grave mistakes.

When we Grow Impatient

The people of Israel grew restless waiting for Moses on the mountain. In their fear and uncertainty, they fashioned a golden calf — something visible, something tangible — to worship. How quickly they forgot the God who had parted seas, who had walked with them in fire and cloud.

This story is not just about idolatry in the past. It's about our own human tendency to fill the silence with something shiny. When answers don't come, when God feels distant, how often do we create our own "golden calves" — habits, distractions, unhealthy attachments — anything to feel in control?

Yet even in their betrayal, God did not abandon His people. There were consequences, yes, but also mercy. There was a chance to turn back.

The Golden Calf reminds us to wait with trust, even when the mountain seems too high and the silence too long. God is still God —even when we cannot yet see what He is doing.

For Spiritual Readers:
- "There's a deeper wisdom at work, even when we can't see it yet."
- "The light doesn't go out, even when the path is dark."
- "The presence that holds us doesn't leave, even when we feel lost."
- "Something greater is still moving, even when we feel stuck."

For More Secular or Non-Religious Readers:
- "Some truths remain steady, even when everything else is changing."
- "Even when things fall apart, there's a centre that can still hold."
- "Life has a way of unfolding meaning, even in or despite the mess."
- "Even when it's quiet, it doesn't mean we're alone."

When it is said that 'God is still God' within the Christian faith, but for anyone, maybe it's enough to trust that some things are still holding us together, even when we don't understand them yet."

Sister's Light
"She understood that moments of failure weren't the end of the story. In her life, understandably, there were times when she felt as though God/His Divine Force had abandoned her. But she had always found that, when she returned to Him, He was there with open arms."

Journalling Invitations

1. **The Israelites turned to a golden calf when they grew impatient with Moses' delay.**
What are some things you have turned to for comfort or security when waiting for God's (or intuitive) direction or provision?
How can you learn to wait patiently and trust in Divine timing?

2. Reflect on moments when fear, impatience, or uncertainty may have led you to seek comfort or control in something other than your faith (whether it was a routine, a relationship, a belief, or a possession). What was driving that need? How did it feel to return to trust in God/your angels/the Divine?

3. **Moses interceded on behalf of the people, asking God for forgiveness.**
Is there someone in your life who needs your prayers and intercession?
How can you stand in the gap for others, especially when they are facing the consequences of their actions?

4. **"How do I respond when I feel God is silent or distant?"**
The Israelites built the calf while Moses was on the mountain, feeling abandoned and unsure. Consider your own times of spiritual waiting. How do you handle that space of silence? What might God be inviting you to learn in those seasons?

5. **The golden calf represents the temptation to turn to false gods when we feel uncertain.**
What are some "idols" in your life that compete for your attention and devotion?
How can you refocus your heart and mind on your spiritual development?

6. **God forgave the Israelites, but they still faced consequences for their sin.**
How do you navigate the tension between forgiveness

and the reality of consequences?

We continue now with the **spying out the Promised Land**, a pivotal moment in the Israelites' journey where fear and faith collide. This story reveals how the Israelites' response to God's promises and their circumstances shaped their future.

The Spies sent to Canaan

Numbers 13-14

After the Israelites had wandered through the wilderness for some time, they finally reached the edge of the Promised Land. God had promised to give them this land, flowing with milk and honey, but before they entered, He commanded Moses to send twelve spies, one from each tribe, to scout out the land as a future home for the Israelite people. The spies were to assess the land's fertility, the strength of its inhabitants, and the condition of its cities.

The twelve spies spent forty days in Canaan, exploring the land and collecting evidence of its abundance. They brought back a large cluster of grapes, so large that it took two men to carry it on a pole between them, along with pomegranates and figs. The land was indeed everything God had promised: fertile, abundant, and rich.

However, when the spies reported back to Moses and the people, ten of them gave a discouraging report. They acknowledged the land's fertility but said, *"The people who live there are powerful, and the cities are fortified and very large. We even saw descendants of Anak there."* The descendants of Anak were giants, and the spies were terrified. They felt as though they were grasshoppers in comparison to the people of the land.

Only Caleb and Joshua spoke differently. Caleb, in particular, stood up and said, *"We should go up and take possession of the land, for we can certainly do it."*

But the people were afraid and began to grumble against Moses and Aaron (his brother), saying, *"If only we had died in Egypt! Or in this wilderness! Why is the Lord bringing us to this land only to let us fall by the sword?"*

The people's lack of faith was evident, and they even began to talk about appointing a new leader to take them back to Egypt. The situation was dire, and God's anger burned against them. Moses and Aaron fell on their faces before the assembly, and Joshua and Caleb tore their clothes in despair. They pleaded with the people, *"The land we passed through and explored is exceedingly good. If the Lord is pleased with us, He will lead us into that land, a land flowing with milk and honey, and will give it to us."*

But the people refused to listen, and they were ready to stone Moses and Aaron to death. At that moment, God's presence appeared at the Tabernacle, and God spoke to Moses, saying, "How long will these people treat me with contempt? How long will they refuse to believe in me, in spite of all the miraculous signs I have performed among them?"

God offered to destroy the people and make a nation from Moses, but Moses interceded for them, reminding God of His promises to Abraham, Isaac, and Jacob. God relented, but He declared that the people who had grumbled and refused to trust Him would not enter the Promised Land. Only Joshua and Caleb, along with the younger generation, would be allowed to enter. The rest of the Israelites would wander in the wilderness for forty more years, one year for each day the spies had spent in Canaan.

Reflection

This moment in Israel's journey highlights a significant lesson about faith versus fear. Despite having seen God's miraculous provision and protection, the people's fear of the giants and fortified cities clouded their ability to trust in God's promises. The fear of the unknown often outweighs the hope that comes with faith, and the Israelites' fear led them to doubt God's ability to bring them into the land He had promised them.

Caleb and Joshua stand out as examples of unwavering trust in God. They saw the giants and the challenges, but their faith in God's power and promises was stronger than their fear. Their courage was rooted in the belief that God had already given them the victory, even if the path seemed impossible.

On the other hand, the ten spies represent the tendency to focus on the obstacles rather than the promises. Fear can cause us to shrink back and lose sight of the bigger picture. When we allow fear to take over, we often miss out on the blessings and victories that God has already prepared for us.

God's response to the people's lack of faith was both just and merciful. Justice was served in the consequences of their rebellion, but mercy was shown in His continued presence with them, despite their unbelief. This story also highlights intercession: Moses' willingness to stand in the gap for the people, pleading for God's mercy. God listened to Moses' plea, showing that even in the face of rebellion, God is open to mercy and forgiveness.

A Sister's Light

"When fear stands in the way, faith has the power to change our perspective. Courage isn't the absence of fear but the trust in our ability to overcome anything we face."

Journalling Invitations

1. **The Israelites saw giants and fortified cities and were overwhelmed by fear.**
What are the "giants" or obstacles in your life that seem impossible to overcome?
How can you change your perspective to focus on God's promises instead of your fears?

2. **Caleb and Joshua trusted God, even when the situation seemed daunting.**
What can you learn from their example of unwavering faith?
How can you cultivate more trust in God's ability to overcome your challenges?

3. **The Israelites wanted to return to Egypt, a place of slavery, because they feared the unknown.**
Are there areas in your life where you are holding on to the "Egypt" of the past because you are afraid of the unknown future?
How can you step forward in faith, trusting that God has better plans for you?

4. **Moses interceded on behalf of the people, asking God for mercy.**

Is there someone you know who needs your intercession or prayers?

How can you advocate for others in times of doubt or fear?

5. The consequences of the Israelites' lack of faith were severe, and they had to wander for forty years.

How do you handle the consequences of your own choices or doubts?

How can you turn back to God when you feel you have missed an opportunity?

6. God remained faithful to His promise, despite the people's lack of trust.

In what ways have you seen God remain faithful to His promises in your life, even when you have doubted?

How can you learn to rely on His faithfulness moving forward?

Let's continue with the **renewal of the covenant** and the powerful display of **God's forgiveness** after the Israelites' rebellion with the golden calf. This part of the journey emphasises God's steadfast love, His willingness to forgive, and the restoration of His relationship with His people.

The Renewal of the Covenant

Exodus 34:1-10

After the Israelites' sin with the golden calf, God's anger was kindled against them, but Moses' intercession led to a moment of mercy. God did not destroy the people but allowed them a path to restoration.

Moses ascended Mount Sinai once again to receive a new set of tablets, as he had broken the original ones in his anger. God told Moses, **"Chisel out two stone tablets like the first ones, and I will write on them the words that were on the first tablets, which you broke."** This act symbolised a fresh start, an opportunity for the Israelites to receive God's forgiveness and recommit to their covenant with Him.

As Moses prepared for the journey up the mountain, God descended in a cloud and revealed His glory to Moses. God proclaimed His name, **"The Lord, the Lord, the compassionate and gracious God, slow to anger, abounding in love and faithfulness, maintaining love to thousands, and forgiving wickedness, rebellion and sin."** This revelation of God's nature was a profound reminder of His goodness and mercy.

God made it clear to Moses that, despite the people's failures, He would **renew His covenant** with them. He was a God who forgives, but He also held the people accountable for their actions. The Israelites were called to renew their commitment to God by remaining faithful and by observing His commands. As Moses came down from the mountain with the new tablets, his face shone with the radiance of God's presence, and the people were in awe of the transformation.

Moses had interceded for the people, and God's forgiveness restored their relationship. The people would continue their journey toward the Promised Land, now with renewed hope and understanding of God's mercy.

Reflection

The story of the renewal of the covenant shows how God's forgiveness is not just about the removal of consequences but about restoration. Even when we fail and make mistakes, God does not abandon us. He offers us the opportunity to begin again, to be restored, and to renew our relationship with Him.

In this story, we see God's character revealed as compassionate, gracious, and forgiving. His nature is not one of quick anger but of slow patience and abundant love. The fact that He is slow to anger shows that He gives us time to repent, to turn back, and to find our way. Even when we stray, He is ready to receive us with open arms.

This moment also highlights the power of intercession. Moses stood before God, pleading for the forgiveness of the people, and through his intercession, they were granted mercy. Intercessory prayer is an act of love and selflessness, standing in the gap for others when they cannot stand for themselves. Moses shows us the heart of a true leader, one who desires not only to see people punished for their wrongs but to see them restored to God.

It is also significant that Moses had to chisel out the new tablets himself. It was not God's fault that the first tablets were broken; it was the people's sin that caused that loss. The act of chiselling out the new tablets symbolises that, while God's forgiveness is free, it sometimes requires effort and sacrifice on our part to make things right.

The Israelites' renewed covenant was a reminder that they were not simply forgiven and then left to continue their lives without change. Restoration comes with a renewed commitment to live according to God's commands. True forgiveness and restoration involve a return to a faithful relationship with God, guided by His Word and His will.

From a philosophical perspective:

A covenant is more than a contract; it is a living relationship, an ongoing commitment between past, present, and future. The renewal of the covenant speaks to the deep human need for reaffirmation, for returning to the promises that shape our identity and purpose.

Philosophically, this renewal invites us to consider the nature of commitment. Are our obligations merely inherited, or do we actively choose them? To renew a covenant is to acknowledge that while time moves forward, meaning must be continually revisited, re-examined, and re-accepted.

It also raises the question of change and continuity. If we are not the same people we were when the covenant was first made, what does it mean to uphold it? Perhaps true renewal is not about rigidly preserving the past, but about finding fresh understanding within an old promise, allowing it to grow as we do.

In our own lives, we make and remake commitments ... to others, to ideals, to ourselves. The real question is not whether we will be faithful to the past, but whether we will engage with it fully in the present, allowing it to guide us into the future.

A Sister's Light

"Mistakes are a part of life. Forgiveness isn't just about erasing those mistakes. It is the opportunity to be made whole again, to walk a different path and to grow into the truest version of yourself."

Journalling Invitations

1. **Moses received new tablets as a symbol of restoration.**

What areas of your life have been broken or marred by mistakes or sin?

How does God's forgiveness/forgiving yourself give you the opportunity for a fresh start?

2. **God revealed His nature to Moses: compassionate, gracious, slow to anger, and abounding in love.**

In what ways can you reflect these characteristics in your relationships with others?

3. **Moses interceded for the people, pleading for God's mercy.**

Who in your life needs your intercession?

How can you stand in the gap for others while encouraging them to grow and find strength within themselves?

4. **Personal Commitments Revisited**

What promises or values have you made to yourself that you may have drifted away from? Reflect on one that still feels important to you today. How might you gently recommit to it with greater awareness and self-compassion?

5. **Seasons of Renewal**

Think of a moment in your life when you felt like you had started fresh (whether by choice or circumstance). What changed in you? How did that 'renewal' shape your current path? Is there anything now that calls for a quiet, meaningful, beginning again?

6. **Forgiveness requires effort, as Moses had to chisel out the new tablets.**

Are there areas in your life where you need to put in effort to make things right?

How can you actively participate in the restoration process in your life and relationships?

The Construction of the Tabernacle

Exodus 35-40

After the Israelites' experience of God's forgiveness, the time had come to build the Tabernacle, a portable sanctuary where God would dwell among His people. The Tabernacle was to be a place of worship, a symbol of God's presence in the midst of the people, and a reminder that He was leading them toward the Promised Land.

God gave Moses detailed instructions on how to build the Tabernacle, which included the Ark of the Covenant, the altar, the lampstand, the altar of incense, and other sacred furnishings. The people were also instructed to contribute materials — gold, silver, bronze, fine linen, and precious stones — to create these sacred items.

Moses then shared these instructions with the Israelites, inviting them to bring their offerings. The people responded with generosity and eagerness, bringing everything needed to construct the Tabernacle. So much was given that Moses had to declare that the people had brought more than enough. It was a beautiful display of community spirit and devotion to God's command.

Skilled craftsmen were appointed to oversee the work, and Bezalel and Oholiab, two men filled with the Spirit of God, were chosen to lead the construction. They crafted each item with great care and precision, following God's exact specifications.

As the work on the Tabernacle was completed, Moses inspected the work, ensuring that everything had been done according to God's command. When the Tabernacle was finally assembled, Moses placed the Ark of the Covenant inside, along with the other sacred items. The cloud of God's presence descended upon the Tabernacle, signifying that God had taken up residence among His people. The Israelites had a visible sign of God's presence: He was now with them in a more intimate and tangible way.

Reflection

The construction of the Tabernacle is a powerful picture of God's desire to dwell with His people. He is not a distant or far-off deity, but one who longs to be in close relationship with us. God's instructions for the Tabernacle were very specific, showing that He values order, beauty, and sacredness in the way we approach Him in worship.

The generosity of the people was a beautiful expression of their gratitude for God's forgiveness and their commitment to worship Him. They understood that their offerings (whether material goods or their time and skills) were an act of worship. Worship is not just about our words or songs; it is about our entire lives, offering what we have to God in service and obedience.

The Spirit of God filling Bezalel and Oholiab was a reminder that God equips His people with the skills and wisdom they need to accomplish His work. God does not call us to tasks without also equipping us to complete them. Whether in creative work or practical service, we are all called to use our talents and gifts for God's glory.

The fact that the cloud of God's presence descended upon the Tabernacle shows that when we obey God and follow His instructions, His presence will dwell with us. Just as the Israelites were given a visible sign of God's presence in the Tabernacle, we, too, are given the Holy Spirit to dwell within us, guiding and empowering us for the journey ahead.

A Broader Reflection on Worship

For someone who is spiritual but not necessarily religious, the word *"worship"* may not centre around formal rituals, hymns, or church services. Instead, it can be understood as **a way of living with intention, reverence, and openness toward something greater than oneself** — whether that is God, the Divine, the sacredness of life, or the interconnectedness of all things

So when we say *"worship is not just about our words or songs; it is about our entire lives,"* it becomes a call to **live mindfully and generously**. To treat others with love. To use our time, gifts, and energy for goodness. To honour life through acts of kindness, integrity, and service.

It's about letting our daily choices (how we listen, how we give, how we forgive) become **offerings** in themselves. In that light, worship becomes less about specific expressions and more about **the posture of the heart**. A way of saying: *"I honour the sacred by how I live."*

From a narrative and symbolic perspective — even when approached without a religious lens — this story represents people coming together with shared intention, creativity, and generosity. Each individual contributed what they could: materials, skills, craftsmanship, and labour. Some spun yarn or worked metal; others carved wood, stitched fabric, or brought precious stones. It was a collaborative act, rooted in a common purpose and the desire to create something meaningful.

A Sister's Light

"It's not about the physical space but about making our hearts a place of worship. When you make room for Him/the Divine in your life, you will see this presence fill every corner, guiding and transforming you."

Journalling Invitations

1. **The Tabernacle was built to be a place where God's presence would dwell.**
How can you make your heart and your life a place where God's presence/Divine presence can reside?

2. **The Israelites gave generously to build the Tabernacle, offering what they had to God.**
What do you have to offer God/your community, whether material, time, or skills?
How can you use your resources to reflect your spiritual beliefs in your life and community?

3. **A Shared Effort**
Think of a time when you were part of a group effort — a project, event, or shared goal. What role did you play?

How did it feel to contribute your part to something bigger than yourself? What did you learn about yourself or others through that experience?

4. The cloud of God's presence filled the Tabernacle, symbolising His closeness to the people.
How have you experienced God's/Divine presence in your own life?
How can you make space to encounter Him more deeply in your daily walk?

5. The Tabernacle required careful attention to detail and obedience to God's instructions.
Are there areas of your life where you are being called to pay attention to the details?
How can you bring greater intentionality and reverence to your worship and/or daily living?

6. The Israelites offered everything they had to build the Tabernacle.
In what ways can you offer more of yourself to be of service in the world?

The **wilderness wanderings** represent a crucial part of the Israelites' journey. Though they had been freed from Egypt, their time in the wilderness was filled with challenges, moments of faithlessness, and God's **faithfulness** in the midst of it all. This time was not just about reaching the Promised Land, but about God shaping the Israelites into a people who would trust and follow Him.

The Wilderness Wanderings

Numbers 10:11-36:13

The Israelites' journey through the wilderness began after the construction of the Tabernacle and the manifestation of God's presence. **For forty years**, the people wandered in the desert, led by God's cloud by day and fire by night. Yet, despite their miraculous escape from Egypt and the presence of God among them, the Israelites continually faced tests of faith.

Their complaints and doubts were frequent. When they ran out of food, God provided **manna from heaven**, and when they were thirsty, He caused water to flow from a rock. Yet, instead of trusting in God's provision, the people often grumbled and wished they had stayed in Egypt. They were **ungrateful** and **impatient**, questioning God's plans for them.

At times, the people's disobedience and rebellion led to severe consequences. One of the most significant instances occurred (as told already) was when they sent **twelve spies** to scout the land of Canaan. Ten spies came back with a negative report, claiming that the land was filled with giants, and the people feared they would not be able to conquer it. Only **Joshua and Caleb** trusted God and believed they could take the land, but the majority rebelled, causing God to declare that the generation that had doubted would not enter the Promised Land. Instead, they would wander for **forty years** until that generation passed away.

Throughout these years, God was teaching the people to trust Him, to rely on His provision, and to obey His commands. He continued to be **patient with them**, even in their rebellion, providing **food**, **water**, and guidance. Yet, He also held them accountable for their actions. There were moments when **God's judgement** came swiftly, as in the case of **Korah's rebellion**, where a group of Israelites rose up against Moses' leadership and were swallowed by the earth as a sign of God's displeasure.

Even so, God's presence remained with the Israelites in the form of the **cloud** that led them, and the **Ark of the**

Covenant that went before them. These signs of His presence and faithfulness reminded the people that He had not abandoned them, even in their most challenging moments.

As the years passed, the Israelites grew from a people who had once lived in slavery to a nation learning to trust in their God. When the **new generation** finally stood at the edge of the Promised Land, they were prepared to enter, having witnessed God's mighty acts of provision and discipline.

Reflection

The wilderness wandering is not only a story of Israel's **physical journey** but a **spiritual journey** that reflects the way we often feel in our own lives. It is easy to become **frustrated** or **doubtful** when faced with the unknown, when we encounter obstacles that seem impossible to overcome, or when the promises of God seem distant. But the wilderness is often where God does His most transformative work. It is a place where we **learn to trust**, where we face our fears, and where we discover that God is **faithful**, even when we are not.

God provided for the Israelites, and He provides for Christians as well. Even in the wilderness seasons of our lives, He offers His **daily provision** whether that comes in the form of **spiritual sustenance**, **guidance**, or **comfort**. The key is whether we choose to trust Him and remain faithful in the face of uncertainty.

The Israelites were constantly called to **remember** God's faithfulness in the wilderness. For us, it is easy to forget God's past faithfulness when we are facing challenges. But looking back at His work in our lives can give us the faith to continue moving forward.

The **rebellion of the people** is a stark reminder of the dangers of **ingratitude** and **disobedience**. When we forget to be grateful for what God has already done, we can easily lose sight of His goodness and fall into **doubt** and **unbelief**. The Israelites' constant grumbling should challenge us to examine our own hearts and attitudes in times of hardship.

Yet, through all the struggles, God remained **faithful**. His presence with the Israelites in the form of the **cloud and fire** is a reminder that He will never leave us, even in our wilderness. He does not forsake His people, and He will provide everything we need, even when it feels like we are wandering in the dark.

From a philosophical perspective:

The wilderness is both a place and a state of being; a space of uncertainty, transition, and self-discovery. The journey is not just about reaching a destination but about who we become along the way.

In the wilderness, old certainties fall away, and new questions emerge. What happens when the familiar is stripped from us? How do we navigate when the path is unclear? The struggle is not only external but internal; a battle between fear and trust, between longing for the past and embracing the unknown.

Perhaps the lesson of the wilderness is that growth requires discomfort. The journey shapes us precisely because it is difficult. It forces us to let go, to redefine ourselves, and to find meaning not in arrival, but in the act of moving forward.

A Sister's Light

*"The wilderness seasons are where we find out who we truly are and who God really is to us. Testing times are never about punishment, but about **purification**. It's in the hard seasons that we learn to trust in God/the Divine more strongly and when we make it through, we come out stronger, more sure of love's presence."'*

Journalling Invitations

1. **The Israelites spent forty years in the wilderness, learning to trust God's provision.**
Have you ever experienced a "wilderness" season in your life?
What did you learn about your own trust in the divine during that time?

2. **Dealing with Doubt and Discontent**
We all experience moments of doubt, frustration, or a sense that life isn't unfolding the way we hoped. Think of a time when you found yourself complaining or feeling uncertain about the path ahead. What was underneath those feelings — fear, unmet needs, exhaustion, something else? How might you meet those moments now with greater understanding or a shift in perspective

3. **God's presence remained with the people in the form of the cloud and fire.**
How have you experienced God's/Divine presence in your own life?
What reminders can you set up to help you stay aware of this in difficult times?

4. **Inner Weather**
Just as the people once grumbled when things felt uncertain, we, too, can be swept up in negativity when we don't see immediate results or clarity. Reflect on a recent time when you were emotionally unsettled — maybe impatient, discouraged, or doubtful. What helped (or could have helped) you steady yourself during that time? What small inner resource might you strengthen to better weather those moments?

5. **Joshua and Caleb trusted God's promises, even when others doubted.**
In what areas of your life do you need to trust more fully?

How can you strengthen your faith when others around you are unsure or fearful?

6. **The Wilderness Within**

Think of a time in your life that felt like a personal "wilderness" — a season of uncertainty, change, or challenge. In what ways did that time shape or prepare you for something that followed? What strengths or insights did you gain from that experience that you carry with you now?

Moving on and the **entry into the Promised Land** represents the culmination of a long journey filled with trials, growth, and faithfulness. It marks the fulfilment of God's promise to Abraham, Isaac, and Jacob, yet it also brings new challenges and lessons for the Israelites. The journey to the Promised Land was not just about a change in geography, but about the transformation of a people, as they learned to walk in God's ways and trust His promises.

The Entry into the Promised Land

Joshua 1-6

After the forty years of wandering in the wilderness, the Israelites finally stood on the edge of the Promised Land, poised to enter and take possession of it. The leader of this new generation was Joshua, a man of great faith and courage, chosen by God to lead the Israelites after Moses' death.

Before crossing into the land, Joshua received a powerful message from God: "Be strong and courageous. Do not be afraid; do not be discouraged, for the Lord your God will be with you wherever you go" (Joshua 1:9). With this reassurance, Joshua led the Israelites across the Jordan River, which miraculously parted as the priests carried the Ark of the Covenant into the water, just as the Red Sea had parted for their ancestors.

The first city they encountered was **Jericho**, a fortified city with high walls that seemed impenetrable. But God gave Joshua specific instructions for conquering it: the Israelites were to march around the city once a day for six days, with the priests carrying the Ark of the Covenant and blowing trumpets. On the seventh day, they were to march around the city seven times, and when the trumpets sounded, the people were to shout.

The Israelites obeyed these seemingly strange instructions, and on the seventh day, as they shouted, the walls of Jericho collapsed. The city was conquered, and the Israelites took possession of the first of many cities in the land.

The victory at Jericho was a clear reminder that God's ways are not always our ways, but when we follow His instructions with faith He brings about victory, even in seemingly impossible situations. It was also a reminder that God's promises are trustworthy, and He is faithful to bring us into the places He has prepared for us, even when the obstacles seem overwhelming.

Reflection

The entry into the Promised Land was a monumental moment for the Israelites, not only because they were entering a new physical land but because it was a new chapter in their relationship with God. **Faith** and **obedience** were key themes in this moment, as the Israelites were called to trust God, even when the path ahead seemed uncertain or difficult.

Joshua's role as leader shows us the importance of **courage** and **trust in God's word**. God gave him the strength to step into a leadership role at a time when the people needed guidance. For us, Joshua's example reminds us that we are never alone in the journeys God calls us to. Even when we feel unprepared, God equips us for the task at hand.

The fall of Jericho highlights the truth that victory comes through obedience, even when God's instructions don't always make sense to us. God often asks us to step out in faith and trust Him in ways that challenge our understanding, but when we obey, He can do the impossible. The Israelites' march around Jericho wasn't a strategy they could have come up with on their own; it was an act of obedience that led to miraculous results.

God's faithfulness in bringing the Israelites into the Promised Land also reminds us of His unchanging nature. No matter what obstacles we face, **God is with us**, guiding us, providing for us, and leading us toward the fulfilment of His promises. Sometimes, the journey is long and filled with hardships, but in the end, God's promises are always worth the wait.

A Spiritual Reflection on the Journey and the Promise

The story of the Israelites reaching the Promised Land speaks to something many of us understand, no matter our background; that life is a journey, often long and winding, full of uncertainty, obstacles, and waiting.

From a spiritual, non-religious standpoint, this story can symbolise our **inner journey toward healing, wholeness, or purpose**. The Promised Land becomes not a place on a map, but a place of peace within us — where we feel aligned, free, and deeply at home.

The "faithfulness of God" in this context might be seen as the **steady presence of the Divine, the Universe, or even the quiet wisdom within** that continues to guide us even when the way forward seems unclear. It reminds us that there is something enduring and trustworthy in the fabric of life, something that helps us keep going when we feel lost.

Though the path may be long, filled with detours and doubts, the journey itself shapes us. And often, in time, we find that what we hoped for (clarity, connection, healing, purpose) arrives. Not always how or when we expected, but in a way that is deeply meaningful.

The promise, then, is not just about arrival; it is about learning to trust the journey, knowing that something sacred is walking with us, within us, and ahead of us.

A Sister's Light

"The journey shapes us and the destination only makes sense when we realise who we've become in the process."'
Inspired by memories of our many conversations

Journalling Invitations

1.   **God told Joshua to be strong and courageous as he led the people into the Promised Land.**
What challenges are you currently facing that require strength and courage?
How can you draw on God's promise/Divine spirit to be with you as you step forward in faith?

2.   **The Israelites crossed the Jordan River on dry ground, just as they had crossed the Red Sea.**
Have you experienced moments when God/your Angels/the Divine made a way for you, even when it seemed impossible?

How can you remember those moments and trust in God's ability to provide for you in future challenges?

3. God's instructions for the conquest of Jericho seemed unconventional, yet the Israelites obeyed.

Are there areas of your life where God is calling you to trust Him with unconventional or unexpected steps?
How can you learn to embrace God's ways, even when they don't make sense to you?

4. The victory at Jericho was a clear demonstration of God's faithfulness.

What victories in your life can you look back on and thank God for?
How has God proven His faithfulness to you in your own journey?

5. Joshua trusted God's word and led the people with courage.

In what areas of your life do you need to trust God's word /your Higher Self more deeply?
How can you step into leadership or take initiative with faith and courage?

6. The Israelites were finally entering the land promised to their ancestors.

What promises of God/intuitive trust in the future are you holding onto in your life?
How can you be patient, faithful, and expectant as you wait for those promises to be fulfilled?

The Division of the Land Among the Tribes

Joshua 13-21

After the miraculous entry into the Promised Land, the Israelites faced the task of dividing the land among the twelve tribes, a momentous occasion that required careful organisation and faith. Each tribe was assigned a specific portion of the land, with the Levites receiving cities scattered throughout the territory, as they did not receive land of their own but were devoted to God's service.

Joshua, under God's direction, oversaw the distribution of the land. This was not merely a political or territorial matter; it was a spiritual act, recognising that the land itself was a gift from God, a part of His covenant with the Israelites. The tribes were to settle in the land, possess it, and honour God with their lives.

This division was an expression of God's faithfulness to His promises to the patriarchs (Abraham, Isaac, and Jacob) and to the generations that had followed. It was a fulfilment of the covenant God had made with His people, a promise to give them a land where they could live and prosper.

But it wasn't all smooth sailing. Even as they began to settle, some tribes struggled with taking full possession of their allotted land. There were still **Canaanite strongholds** in certain areas, and some tribes were hesitant or unwilling to completely drive out the inhabitants. Despite this, God continued to remind His people that He would be with them, and that **obedience to His commands** was the key to their success in maintaining the land.

One of the most significant elements of this time was the **cities of refuge**: six cities designated as places where anyone who had committed manslaughter could flee for safety. These cities were symbols of God's mercy, offering protection to those who might otherwise face vengeance. The cities of refuge provided a picture of God's justice and mercy working together, ensuring that those who were guilty of accidental harm had a place to find sanctuary while they awaited trial.

In the division of the land, God's promises were not just fulfilled in a **material** sense but in a deeper, more spiritual way. The land represented the place where the Israelites were to live out their covenant relationship with God. It was a place where they were to build a **holy community**, honouring God through their worship, obedience, and actions.

Reflection

The division of the land was a pivotal moment in Israel's history, a moment when God's promise came to fruition, and His people were called to take responsibility for the land He had given them. It was a reminder that the blessings God provides come with responsibility; the Israelites were entrusted with the land, but they had to care for it, protect it, and honour God in the midst of it.

For Christians, this story speaks of the idea that God's blessings in our lives come with a call to faithfulness. We are entrusted with gifts (whether they be spiritual, material, or emotional) and we are called to steward them well, using them for God's purposes. Just as the Israelites were given the land to possess and care for, we are given many areas of our lives that we are meant to steward and honour God with.

The cities of refuge stand as a powerful reminder of God's mercy and justice. Just as the Israelites were given places to find refuge, we can find refuge in God's mercy when we fall short. He provides a safe place for us, even when we make mistakes, and calls us to extend that same mercy to others.

The struggle of some tribes to fully take possession of their land also serves as a warning. We are called to claim and take hold of the promises God has for us, not leaving any part of our inheritance unclaimed. There may be moments when we face resistance, doubt, or fear, but God's promises are meant to be fully realised, and He will be with us as we walk in faith.

From a spiritual perspective, through this story we are invited to step fully into the potential and purpose life holds for us, embracing the inner wisdom, strength, and joy that are our birthright. There may be times when uncertainty, fear, or self-doubt cloud our path ... but the deep truths meant for us, the ones that resonate with our spirit, are not meant to be half-lived or left behind. As we move forward with trust in the unfolding journey, we find that we are never truly alone. Life itself, with all its mystery and beauty, supports our becoming.

A Sister's Light
"The journey isn't just about finding peace but about holding onto it and honouring it every day."

Journalling Invitations

1. **The land was a gift, but it came with the responsibility to steward it.**
What blessings in your life require stewardship? Have you ever inherited something (a space, a responsibility, a role) that came with unspoken expectations? How did it shape your choices or identity?

2. **Some tribes were reluctant to fully take possession of their land.**
Are there areas in your life where you've hesitated to fully embrace what has been given you? What does "belonging" to a place mean to you? Reflect on a time when a physical or emotional boundary helped define your sense of home (or challenged it).

3. **Fairness and Distribution**
When you think about how resources like land, time, or opportunity are divided in the world around you, what feelings come up? What does fairness look like to you in a community setting?

4. **God's promise to give the land was a part of the covenant.**
Reflect on a time when a promise (spoken or unspoken) was tied to a place or a shared goal. This could be a family agreement, a personal commitment, or a community vision. How did that promise shape your relationship to the space or the people involved? Have you ever made a personal "covenant" with yourself tied to a certain place or chapter in life?

5.   Joshua led the people to claim the land, but it was up to the tribes to settle in it.
Reflect on a shared space in your life — perhaps a garden, home, workspace, or even a memory shared with others. What made it work well, or what tensions existed within it?

6.   The land was not only about physical possession, but spiritual obedience.
Where in your life are you being called to "claim your space"? This could be physical, emotional, creative, or relational. What would it look like to step into that space fully?

The final chapter of the Israelites' journey into the Promised Land is a time of renewal, commitment, and reflection. It's a moment where the people look back at how far they've come, recognise the faithfulness of God, and renew their covenant with Him as they prepare for the next phase of life in the land. This chapter emphasises the importance of choosing to follow God and remaining faithful, not just in times of victory, but throughout all seasons of life.

Joshua's Farewell and Covenant Renewal

Joshua 23-24

As Joshua grew old and approached the end of his life, he gathered the Israelite leaders together for a final speech. He wanted to ensure that the people understood the importance of remaining faithful to God, who had brought them to this moment.

Joshua reminded them of God's goodness, recounting all the ways in which He had delivered them, fought for them, and fulfilled His promises. He emphasised that the Israelites were to continue serving the Lord with all their heart, choosing to follow Him and not be swayed by the idols and gods of the surrounding nations. He challenged them to take responsibility for their relationship with God and to commit to serving Him alone.

Joshua famously said, *"But as for me and my household, we will serve the Lord"* (Joshua 24:15). This declaration was a powerful testimony to his commitment to God, and it became a model for the people. He asked them to make the same commitment: to choose this day whom they would serve.

The people responded by declaring their allegiance to the Lord, acknowledging His greatness and His work in their lives. Joshua then made a covenant with them, a renewed promise to serve and follow God. He set up a stone as a witness to the covenant, a tangible reminder of the commitments they had made.

Joshua's farewell was a **call to faithfulness**. He urged the people to remember God's promises and to live in obedience to His commands, knowing that their success in the Promised Land depended on their continued devotion to God.

After Joshua's death, the Israelites would go on to face many challenges in the land, but the foundation for their success was laid in their **commitment** to God's ways. The covenant renewal was a **new beginning**, a chance for the people to embrace their inheritance and the calling to be a light to the nations.

Reflection

Joshua's final words to the Israelites carry powerful lessons for us today. The covenant renewal reminds us of the importance of regularly choosing to follow God, especially in moments of transition or after experiencing great victories. It's easy to become complacent or distracted by the world around us, but we are called to intentionally commit to God each day, just as the Israelites did in the land they had been promised.

The Israelites' decision to renew their covenant with God is an invitation to us to ask ourselves: Who are we serving today? We may not face the same physical challenges that the Israelites did, but we face the daily decision of whether we will serve the Lord with our whole hearts or let other distractions take precedence. God's call to faithfulness is not limited to a specific time or place, it is a call to live with integrity and devotion in every moment of life.

Joshua's declaration, **"As for me and my household, we will serve the Lord,"** is a powerful statement of **intentionality** and **commitment**. It challenges us to lead our families, communities, and ourselves in a **purposeful** and **faithful** way. It also highlights the importance of being **a witness** to others, showing them the path to faithfulness, just as Joshua did.

In many ways, the **covenant renewal** is an invitation to us to ask: What does it mean to serve the Lord in our lives today? How can we be intentional in our faithfulness, choosing God over other distractions and challenges?

Joshua's death marked the end of an era, but his example of **faithfulness** and **obedience** remained. The Israelites would continue to face trials, but the foundation for their life in the Promised Land was laid in their commitment to the Lord. For us, this is a reminder that our lives, too, are shaped by the choices we make to follow God. The journey isn't over when we reach the promised places in our lives; it's just the beginning of a new chapter where **faithfulness** continues to be the key.

Choose What Grounds You

At the end of his life, Joshua gathered the people and invited them to remember. He spoke of where they had come from (through wilderness, through hardship) and reminded them of the faithfulness that had carried them.

Then he asked them to choose:

"Choose this day whom you will serve... But as for me and my house, we will serve the Lord." (Joshua 24:15)

Even for those not following a religious tradition, this moment speaks to something universal. We all come to crossroads where we must ask: *What will I stand for? What will I carry forward? What will I release?*

Joshua's farewell is a call to live with intention. It reminds us that life is not just something that happens to us, it's something we shape with our choices. He invites the people to root themselves in something deeper than fear or convenience.

For you, it may not be about serving God in the traditional sense. But it might be about choosing integrity, choosing love, choosing to be faithful to what matters most.

In the end, the question is simple and enduring: *What will guide you when life gets uncertain?*

The Journey of Faithful Covenant

Joshua's final words, "As for me and my household, we will serve the Lord," are an invitation to each of us to make that same declaration in our own lives. It's a call to lead not just with our words, but with our hearts and actions. It's a challenge to remain **committed** to God/Love/the Divine not only when the journey is easy but through every moment, whether in joy or hardship, in victory or struggle.

As we close this part of the story, let us remember that we are all on a journey of **covenant**, a journey that calls for ongoing faithfulness, **trust** in God's/Divine guidance, and the courage to choose, just as the Israelites did.

A Sister's Light

"She believed that our moments of transition (whether in joy or hardship) are opportunities to re-establish our faith in the Universe."

Journalling Invitations

1.   Joshua asked the Israelites to choose whom they would serve.
What drives you? What guides your decisions? Who or what are you giving your life to? This isn't about worship: it's about *choice* and *alignment*. It's a reminder that we have the power to decide what we stand for and to live in a way that reflects those decisions with clarity and purpose.

2.   Joshua's statement, "As for me and my household, we will serve the Lord," was a personal declaration.
This statement invites reflection on what values or principles you choose to live by and how these shape your environment and relationships. If you were to make a personal declaration about how you intend to live, what would it say? How do your actions reflect that intention in your daily life or home?

3.   The Israelites made a covenant with God, renewing their commitment to Him.
What promises or commitments do you want to re-establish today?

4.   The stone that Joshua set up served as a witness to the covenant.
What tangible reminders can you set up in your life to help you in your spiritual development? How can you stay rooted in faith when distractions or difficulties arise?

5.   Joshua's farewell speech emphasised the importance of remembering God's faithfulness.
Take some time to reflect on the importance of remembering the sources of strength, support, and guidance that have helped you through life's challenges. Looking back on your life so far, what has sustained you through the hardest times? What people, inner

strengths, or life lessons do you want to remember and carry forward?

6. Joshua called the people to be faithful in all things.

What does being "faithful" mean to you in everyday life? Are there areas where you strive to show up consistently and with integrity? Reflect on a time when you stayed true to something or someone despite difficulty. How did that shape you? What helps you remain grounded in what matters most to you?

We will now move on to David. His journey is rich with themes of **faith**, **obedience**, **repentance**, and **transformation**. Let's begin with the first part of his story — his **anointing as king** — and how this moment marks the beginning of his journey.

☽✦ Handwritten Reflections ✦☽

You are invited to sit quietly with what you've read. Below is space for your own thoughts, prayers, or dreams that rise as you ponder these bible stories and their meaning in your life.

✏ _____

✏ _____

✏ _____

✏ _____

✏ _____

✏ _____

✏ _____

✏ _____

✹ *"The heavens declare the glory of God; the skies proclaim the work of His hands." — Psalm 19:1* ✹
Let these pages be your sacred sky.

David Anointed as King
1 Samuel 16:1-13

The story begins with a pivotal moment in the life of **David**, when he is anointed as king over Israel by the prophet **Samuel**. At the time, the people had rejected God's leadership and demanded a king like the other nations. God had allowed Saul to be king, but Saul's disobedience led to God's rejection of him as king. God sent Samuel to the house of **Jesse**, a man from the tribe of Judah, to anoint one of his sons as the new king.

When Samuel arrived at Jesse's house, he saw the older sons and assumed one of them would be chosen. However, God spoke to Samuel, saying, "**Do not look at his appearance or at the height of his stature, because I have rejected him. For the Lord does not see as man sees; for man looks at the outward appearance, but the Lord looks at the heart**" (1 Samuel 16:7).

After seeing all of Jesse's sons, Samuel asked if there were any others. Jesse then called in David, the youngest, who was tending the sheep. As soon as Samuel saw David, God told him, "**Arise, anoint him; for this is the one**" (1 Samuel 16:12). Samuel anointed David in front of his brothers, and from that day on, the **Spirit of the Lord came upon David** in a powerful way.

Reflection

David's anointing marks the beginning of his transformation from a humble shepherd boy to the future king of Israel. What stands out in this story is how **God sees the heart** rather than outward appearances. David wasn't the strongest or the most impressive by worldly standards, but he was chosen because of the goodness in his heart.

In many ways, this story speaks of the **journey of identity and calling**. Like David, we often don't see the full picture of our lives from the outside. But God looks at our hearts, our desires, and our willingness to serve Him, even in the smallest of tasks. David was faithful in the field, tending sheep, when God saw his potential to lead a nation.

This moment is a strong reminder that God's calling is not determined by external factors or human expectations. He calls us because of what is in our hearts ... our willingness to follow His lead, no matter where we are or what we're doing. David's heart of worship, humility, and obedience prepared him to take on the monumental role of king.

Reflection on the Power of Being Seen

When the prophet Samuel was sent to anoint the next king, he expected to find someone outwardly powerful, tall, strong, and impressive. But God led him to a shepherd boy named David, overlooked by everyone except for God. David wasn't the obvious choice, but he was the one who would lead with a heart of courage and compassion.

There are times in our lives when we find ourselves questioning our own worth or place in the world. Sometimes, we think we need to be someone else to be worthy of the role we've been called to, whether that's leadership, love, or simply living with integrity. We may feel "too small" or "too unnoticed." But David's story reminds us that greatness is often found in the quiet spaces; the unseen, uncelebrated places where true strength and wisdom grow.

The world may miss us, but we are always seen by what truly matters. What if our most significant qualities are not the ones the world applauds, but the ones that come from within — our hearts, our values, and our quiet determination?

A Sister's Light

"What matters is what is in our hearts; not our limitations. It is the way we behave in the quiet, unseen moments. It is our deepest beliefs and the love we share with the world that shapes us for what is to come."

Journalling Invitations

1. **God saw David's heart and chose him despite outward appearances.**
Reflect on a time when you felt overlooked or underestimated. How did this experience to shape you

or prepare you for something greater?

How can you nurture a hear that stays open to your true purpose, even when others may not recognise your potential?

2. **David was chosen while doing something humble ... tending sheep.**

What small, everyday tasks in your life might be shaping your character or preparing you for something greater? How can you approach these moments with care, dedication, and a willingness to grow?

3. **David was anointed with the Spirit of the Lord.**

What does it mean to you to be equipped with inner wisdom and strength for the path you're meant to walk? Take a quiet moment to reflect on the guidance you've received along the way, and how you've been prepared — often in unseen ways — for the journey ahead.

4. **Samuel had to trust God's judgement over his own perception of what a king should look like.**

Is there an area in your life where you're being challenged to trust a wisdom beyond your own understanding? How might you release rigid ideas of success or self-worth to align more closely with a deeper sense of purpose and truth?

5. **David's story is one of growth, transformation, and destiny.**

In what ways do you sense life shaping you for something meaningful? How can you learn to trust this feeling even when the road ahead feels uncertain or unclear?"

This marks the beginning of **David's story**, but it's just the start of his path of faithfulness, trials, and eventual kingship

David and Goliath

1 Samuel 17:1-51

The story of David and Goliath is one of the most well-known in the Bible. The Philistine army faced off against Israel, and in their ranks stood Goliath, a giant warrior who taunted Israel's soldiers for forty days. He challenged any Israelite to fight him, but no one dared to accept. Goliath's size, strength, and reputation filled the Israelites with fear.

At this time, David was still a young shepherd, sent by his father, Jesse, to deliver food to his older brothers who were serving in Saul's army. When David heard Goliath's taunting, he was deeply moved. He questioned why no one was stepping forward to defend the honour of God's name.

David's faith was unwavering. He believed that God had delivered him from danger before, when he fought off a lion and a bear while protecting his sheep. He saw this battle with Goliath not as his own fight, but as a fight for God's glory. When King Saul heard of David's willingness to fight, he tried to offer David his armour, but David refused, choosing instead to go with only his staff, five smooth stones, and his slingshot.

David approached Goliath with bold faith, declaring, "*You come against me with sword and spear, but I come against you in the name of the Lord Almighty*" (1 Samuel 17:45). With a single stone, David struck Goliath in the forehead, and the giant fell. David's victory was not just over Goliath, but a declaration that God's power was greater than human strength. David's faith led him to triumph in what seemed to be an impossible situation.

Reflection

The story of David and Goliath reflects the courage that comes from trusting in God's strength, even when the odds seem insurmountable. David, though young and inexperienced in battle, had the faith that God would equip him for the task at hand. The key moment is when David says to Goliath, "*I come against you in the name of the Lord Almighty*." This is a reminder that our faith is not based on our abilities or resources, but on God's power working through us.

David's victory invites us to examine our own fears and personal 'giants' ... whether they are external challenges, inner struggles, or doubts that hold us back. Goliath can symbolise anything that feels overwhelming or beyond our control. Yet David's story reminds us that courage, trust in a greater purpose, and staying true to our values can lead to triumph. It's not about having all the strength, but about facing fears with courage, clarity, and conviction

David's courage wasn't born from a lack of fear, but from faith in God's faithfulness in past battles. He remembered how God had been with him in the past, and he trusted that God would be with him in this moment. The same applies to us: as we encounter challenges, we can draw strength from past experiences of resilience and trust that we will be equipped to handle whatever lies ahead.

Facing the Giants Within

The story of David and Goliath is one of the most well-known tales of unlikely victory. A young shepherd, with no armour and only a simple sling, defeats a giant warrior that everyone else feared. This is a scene of courage, not because David was physically stronger, but because he saw something others didn't. This demonstrates the power of confidence, determination, and belief in a cause greater than oneself.

For many of us, Goliath is not a literal giant; he relates to the challenges we face, the doubts that overwhelm us, or the fears that seem insurmountable. It is easy to feel small in the face of big problems, like we have nothing to offer. But David's story invites us to consider: What if the "giants" we face are not as powerful as we imagine? What if, like David, we have resources inside us (resilience, ingenuity, quiet courage) that are enough to overcome what feels impossible?

David didn't fight with the tools others thought he needed. He used what he knew best. This reminds us that the power to face our own giants might already lie within us, in our personal strengths, our unique talents, and in the wisdom we've gained through life's challenges.

A Sister's Light

"The giants we face in life are often the ones that appear the most daunting and unmovable, but we don't have to fight our battles alone."

Journalling Invitations

1. **David faced Goliath with faith in God's power.**
Think back to a time in your life when you faced a challenge that felt insurmountable. What helped you move through that experience, and what inner or outer strength supported you? What 'giants' are you facing now, and how might you draw on resilience, trust, or a greater sense of purpose to face them?

2. **David trusted in God's past faithfulness.**
Think back on moments when life seemed to offer you quiet reassurance or unexpected support — even in small ways. How can remembering those times help you build confidence and trust when facing future challenges? How might you continue to hold on to hope and inner strength, even when the outcome is still unclear?

3. **David didn't rely on worldly armour or strength, but on God's power.**
Are there areas of your life where you're carrying the weight alone, relying solely on your own strength? What might it look like to move forward with trust — in God, in something greater than yourself, or in the quiet wisdom that life offers, especially in the challenges you're facing now

4. **David's victory was for God's glory.**
How might you change your perspective when facing challenges ... viewing them not just as personal struggles, but as opportunities for growth, courage, and integrity? In what ways can you move through life's

battles, both big and small, in a way that reflects your deepest values and brings light to those around you?

5.   **David's faith was bold and fearless.**

Take a little time now to pray for boldness in your own faith. What areas of your life do you need to bring before God and ask for courage and confidence, just like David?

This chapter in David's journey is a great example of **faith**, **courage**, and **obedience**. It challenges us to **trust God's/Divine power** over our own limitations and to face our fears with confidence. We are not alone.

David's Flight from Saul

1 Samuel 18:17-30; *19:1-24; 21:1-15;22;24*

After David defeated **Goliath**, he quickly rose to prominence in Israel. **King Saul**, initially pleased with David's bravery and success, became increasingly jealous as David's popularity grew. Saul's jealousy turned to hatred and fearful that David might take his throne, he began plotting to kill David.

In 1 Samuel 18:17-30, Saul tried to kill David on multiple occasions, both through direct attempts on his life and by setting him up in dangerous situations. Despite Saul's efforts, David's popularity only grew, and he formed a close bond with Jonathan, Saul's son, who warned him of his father's intentions.

This marked the beginning of David's years as a fugitive, constantly running from Saul.

In **1 Samuel 19**, Saul openly orders his servants to kill David. But **Jonathan** helps him escape, even rebuking his father for his unjust anger. David flees and finds temporary refuge with the prophet **Samuel**. Saul tried to send men to capture David, but each time they encountered Samuel and his prophets, they were overwhelmed by the Spirit of God and could not complete the mission.

David spent much time fleeing from Saul, seeking refuge in various places, including the wilderness of Ziph and the stronghold of Engedi. During this period, David gathered a group of loyal followers. Despite his fear and the constant threat of death, David showed restraint, even sparing Saul's life when he had the opportunity to kill him.

David continues his flight and eventually seeks refuge in Gath, the territory of the Philistines, where he feigns madness to avoid being recognised.

David's flight from Saul is a story of survival, resilience, and the struggle between fear and faith. Throughout his years of fleeing, David learned deep lessons about trust, leadership, and patience. Despite the danger, David trusted in a greater purpose, knowing that, in time, he would be called to lead Israel.

Reflection

David's flight from Saul offers reflection on the **trial of trust**. David did not understand why Saul turned against him, nor did he see the end of the road when he fled from place to place. However, his trust in God remained constant. He could have taken matters into his own hands, tried to overthrow Saul, or become bitter and angry. But David chose to wait on God's timing and trust in His plan, even when it seemed uncertain.

David's experience in the wilderness also highlights the theme of **refuge**. He was constantly seeking places of safety, but more importantly, he was seeking refuge in **God**. His psalms during this time reflect his longing for God's presence and his unwavering belief that **God was his protector**. Even in the midst of peril, David knew that God was faithful and would not forsake him.

This part of David's story encourages us to trust in God's/Divine protection and provision when we find ourselves in **seasons of trial and uncertainty**. It reminds us that even when life is challenging and the future uncertain, there is a greater force of guidance at work. Just as David found his way through difficult times, we too can find direction and strength to navigate our own wilderness experiences.

David was anointed as the future king, yet instead of immediate glory, he found himself hunted by the very ruler he had once served loyally. This paradox invites reflection: Why does a divine calling often lead first to suffering? It suggests that the path to fulfilling one's purpose is not paved with ease but with trials that shape character and deepen faith. David's exile was not merely an escape; it was a crucible where his trust in God was tested and refined.

Saul's relentless pursuit of David reveals the consuming nature of fear. Though Saul was still king, he was haunted by the knowledge that he had lost divine favour. His actions reflect how insecurity can lead a person to destruction, turning them against even those who wish them no harm. In contrast,

David chose to spare Saul's life multiple times, embodying restraint and humility. This contrast presents a meditation on leadership: true strength is not in dominance but in moral courage and trust in a higher justice.

David's time in the wilderness mirrors the journeys of many biblical figures (Moses, Elijah, and even Jesus) who faced trials in desolate places before stepping into their full purpose. The wilderness is both a place of danger and divine encounter, where dependence on God becomes absolute. How often in our own lives do we experience exile of sorts ... times of uncertainty, displacement, or fear? Like David, we may find that these moments, painful as they are, strip away illusions and prepare us for something greater.

A Sister's Light

"In the hardest seasons of life, we can't always see the path ahead, but we can trust that God is leading us, even in the dark. She reminded me that sometimes waiting is part of the journey and that waiting with faith and trusting in the process is where we find God's/Divine's presence the most."

Journalling Invitations

1. **David's flight was filled with uncertainty and danger.**
Reflect on a time in your life when you faced uncertainty or challenge. How did you experience a sense of guidance or support during that time? How can you cultivate trust in God/in something greater than yourself when the path ahead is unclear?

2. **David did not try to take matters into his own hands but chose to wait on God.**
Is there an area of your life where you're struggling to wait for the right timing? How can you let go of the need to control the outcome and trust that there is a bigger plan unfolding, even if it's not yet clear?

3.   **David sought refuge in God, even as he faced physical dangers.**

How do you find a sense of refuge and strength during difficult times?

Take a moment to pray, asking God to be your refuge and strength in any challenges you may be facing.

4.   **David's faith remained strong even when he was on the run.**

What are some ways you can nurture and strengthen your inner resilience during times of trial or waiting? How can you hold onto hope, even when the future seems uncertain?

5.   **David's honesty in his pain and struggle can be seen in his psalms.**

Do you feel free to be honest about your struggles?

Take a moment to write or pray out your own feelings of frustration, fear, or uncertainty.

David's time in the wilderness, fleeing from Saul, teaches us that even in the hardest seasons, we are not alone, and we can find strength within ourselves and through our faith. David's journey through this period is marked by his refusal to give in to bitterness or despair, instead choosing to trust in the unfolding of a greater plan.

David's Rise to Kingship and Saul's Death

2 Samuel 1:1-27; 2:1-7; 5:1-5

After many years of running from King Saul, David's time of waiting was finally coming to an end. Saul and his son Jonathan died in battle against the Philistines. When news of their deaths reached David, he mourned deeply, showing great respect and sorrow for Saul, his former king, and for Jonathan, his dear friend. In 2 Samuel 1, David composes a beautiful and heartfelt lament for Saul and Jonathan, expressing both his grief and his admiration for the man who had once been his king.

Though Saul had tried to kill him, David still honoured the position that Saul held as God's anointed king. His grief over Saul's death demonstrates David's humility, even in the face of deep personal betrayal.

After Saul's death, David was anointed king over Judah in Hebron, while the rest of Israel remained loyal to Saul's son Ishbosheth. The struggle for the throne continued, as Ishbosheth's reign was challenged by the forces of David's army, led by Joab. Over time, David's kingdom grew, and God gave him victory over his enemies.

Eventually, all of Israel came to David, recognising him as the rightful king. In 2 Samuel 5, David is anointed king over all of Israel and establishes Jerusalem as his capital, fulfilling God's promise to him. He reigns for forty years: seven years over Judah, and then thirty-three years over all of Israel. His reign is marked by military victories, a desire to bring the Ark of the Covenant to Jerusalem, and to build a house for God.

David's rise to kingship, however, was not immediate. It came after years of **patience**, **perseverance**, and trusting in God's timing. Though David had been anointed by Samuel many years earlier, it was God's timing (not David's) that determined when he would officially step into his role as king.

Reflection

David's journey to the throne is a testament to **God's sovereignty** and **perfect timing**. It is easy to grow impatient in seasons of waiting, especially when the promise feels far off or when circumstances seem to work against us. David had been promised the throne, yet he had to endure years of hardship and injustice before seeing that promise fulfilled.

In these years of waiting, David learned **humility** and **honour**, even in difficult circumstances. His ability to mourn Saul's death, despite Saul's attempts to kill him, shows a heart of **integrity**. He did not seek revenge or delight in the downfall of his enemy. Instead, he honoured the position that Saul once held and grieved over the loss of the man who had once been a father figure to him.

David's story teaches Christians that **God's timing is always right**, even when we cannot see the end of the road. David's faithfulness during his time of waiting was a key factor in his eventual success. His rise to the throne came when God had fully prepared him for it, not a moment sooner. This story invites us to trust that there is a greater force at work behind the scenes, even when we cannot see the full picture.

David's rise to kingship and Saul's death reveal the fragile nature of power and the divine rhythm of destiny. Saul, once chosen, fell not by David's hand but by the weight of his own fear and disobedience, reminding us that grasping too tightly to control often leads to ruin. David, on the other hand, ascended not through conquest but through patience, suffering, and faith, teaching us that true leadership is not seized; it is received in its appointed time. His story invites us to trust in the unfolding of our own purpose, even when the path is uncertain.

A Sister's Inspiration
"The waiting seasons are never wasted. We are being prepared for something greater in our waiting. Don't rush it. God/the Universe is making sure you are ready for what's next."

Journalling Invitations

1. **David's rise to kingship came after years of waiting and uncertainty.**
Reflect on a time when you were waiting for something important, and it felt like the promise was delayed. How did you experience a sense of support and reassurance during that waiting period? How can you learn to trust in the timing of life, especially in the areas where you feel impatient or uncertain?

2. **David honoured Saul, even after Saul tried to kill him.**
Is there someone in your life whom you struggle to respect due to past hurt or betrayal?
How can you choose to value others, even in difficult circumstances, knowing that your intentions are seen and appreciated, and that doing so will bring a sense of fulfilment and respect in return?

3. **David's path to the throne was marked by humility and integrity.**
Are there areas of your life where you may be tempted to take shortcuts or act out of impatience?
How can you grow in humility and integrity, trusting that your path will unfold in its own time,

4. **David's success came not through his own strength, but through God's provision.**
Take a moment to reflect on the ways in which God has provided for you in your life especially in times when

you didn't expect it.

How can you recognise God's provision in your current situation, and how can you express gratitude for His faithfulness?

5. **David's reign was marked by both victories and struggles.**

What victories have you experienced in your life, and how can you use those moments of success to inspire or uplift others? How can you remain resilient in the face of challenges, trusting that you are supported through every season?

David's journey from **fugitive** to **king** was filled with challenges, yet it was through these challenges that he was shaped into the leader God intended him to be. His story is one of **faithfulness**, **humility**, and **trust** in God's timing. As we reflect on David's rise to kingship, we are reminded that **God is faithful** to fulfil His promises in His perfect time.

Let's continue with the next chapter in David's journey; his desire to build a temple for God and God's covenant with David. This chapter reveals David's heart for God and highlights the promise God made to him, as well as the faith that David exhibited.

David's Desire to build the Temple and God's Covenant
2 Samuel 7:1-29

After David was established as king and had experienced both great victories and deep personal struggles, he settled into a period of peace in his kingdom. He looked around at his palace, a grand structure, and then at the **Ark of the Covenant**, which was housed in a tent. David felt that it was wrong that he lived in a beautiful palace, while the Ark, the symbol of God's presence, remained in a humble tent. Deeply moved by this, David decided to build a permanent temple for God, a house worthy of God's presence.

David shared his desire with the prophet Nathan, who initially encouraged him to go ahead with his plans. However, that very night, God spoke to Nathan, telling him to go back to David with a message. God revealed that David, though a man after God's own heart, would not be the one to build the temple. Instead, God had other plans and **David's son, Solomon**, would be the one to build the temple.

Yet, in this conversation, God made a covenant with David that would change the course of history. God promised David that his dynasty would endure forever, and that his descendants would sit on the throne of Israel. This was a promise that pointed not only to Solomon but also to **Jesus Christ**, who would come from the line of David and establish an eternal kingdom.

David, overwhelmed by God's faithfulness, responded with a heartfelt prayer of gratitude. He acknowledged that God had chosen him and his family to carry out this great work and that God's plans were far greater than anything David could have imagined. David's desire to build a house for God was noble, but God's plan for his family was even more glorious; a promise of an eternal kingdom that would eventually be fulfilled through Jesus Christ, the ultimate descendant of David.

Reflection

David's desire to build the temple came from a place of deep **love** and **reverence** for God. He wanted to honour God by providing a permanent home for the Ark. But God's response revealed that David's role in God's plan was different than what he had expected. David wasn't discouraged or disappointed by this change in plans. Instead, he humbly accepted it and continued to trust in God's bigger picture.

This story reveals the importance of **trusting in God's timing** and His plans, even when they differ from our own. David's heart for God was evident, and though he wasn't able to fulfil the dream of building the temple, God still honoured him with an everlasting promise. Sometimes, our desires and plans may not come to fruition in the way we expect, but if we can go with the flow, we might find that His plan is always better than our own.

David's response is also a reminder of the importance of **worship**. Even when things don't go as planned, David continued to honour God through worship, trusting that God's purposes were being fulfilled in ways he might not fully understand. His life teaches us that we can trust God even when we don't know the full picture, faith is the key to fulfilling God's plan for our lives.

So, at times we might decide to take on certain tasks or roles, only to find that **God has a different plan** ... one that might not always align with our initial desires. Yet, even when God redirects us, His plans for us are filled with **hope**, **purpose**, and **glory**.

David's response to God's refusal to let him build the temple is key. Instead of feeling discouraged, he responded with humility and gratitude. He understood that it was an honour simply to be part of God's plan, even if it wasn't exactly what he had envisioned. This response teaches us the importance of surrendering our plans to God/the Divine and trusting that it will turn out okay.

God's promise to David that his **descendants would rule forever** is ultimately fulfilled in the person of **Jesus Christ**, the eternal King. David's faithfulness and humility set the stage for the **coming Messiah**, reminding us that **our faithfulness** to God, even in small things, can play a significant role in His larger story.

From a neutral perspective

David's desire to build a temple for God reflects a deep yearning to honour the divine, yet God's response reveals that sometimes our highest aspirations are not aligned with divine will. While David's heart was pure, the temple was not meant to be his work, but that of his son Solomon, showing that not all good desires are meant to be fulfilled in our time. This interaction highlights a profound truth: God's covenant with David was not about human effort, but about divine promise; God's plans often unfold in ways that transcend our understanding, calling us to trust in a greater purpose beyond our own ambitions.

A Sister's Light

"Sometimes the most important thing is not what we do, but how we respond when our plans change. Trust there is a 'reason' behind everything and that God/the Divine's vision for you is greater than your own. She felt her accident was meant to be; it shaped her character and strengthened her faith. When the path changes, know that this is part of a bigger story."

Journalling Invitations

1. **David had a heart to build a house for God, but God had a bigger plan.**
Reflect on a time when you felt a strong desire to pursue something important, but your plans were redirected. How did you respond? How can you embrace a larger, unforeseen plan for your life, even when it differs from what you originally envisioned?

2. **God promised David that his descendants would rule forever.**
Think about the promises you've held onto in your life. How can you trust in them, even when they haven't yet

come to fruition? What aspects of past commitments or moments of trust remind you of the resilience and faithfulness you've experienced

For Christians: What aspects of God's covenant with David remind you of His faithfulness to you?

3. **David's humility and gratitude in response to God's plans were striking.**

When things don't go as planned, how do you respond? How can you grow in humility and trust, like David, recognising that life's unfolding may serve your deeper good — even when the path looks different from what you expected?

4. **David acknowledged that God's plans were far greater than his own.**

Are there areas of your life where you're still holding tightly to your own plans, even though life may be leading you in a different direction? How can you begin to release control and trust in the possibility of a greater purpose unfolding for you?

5. **David's response was one of awe and praise.**

For Christians: Take a moment to reflect on God's faithfulness in your life. What are you thankful for? Spend time in prayer, praising God for His plans and promises, trusting that He is working in ways you may not fully understand yet.

David's desire to build a temple for God and the covenant God made with him are reminders that God's plans are always bigger than our own. Through David's humility, gratitude, and trust in God's timing, we see an example of how to approach life with a patient heart even when the path is different to how we imagined it would be. God's promises to David are also a reminder that, though we may not always see the final outcome, His faithfulness endures through all generations.

Let's continue now with the story of David's sin with Bathsheba and the consequences that followed focusing on how David's choices led to a profound impact not only on his own life but also on the lives of others.

Carole Somerville

David's Sin with Bathsheba and its Consequences

2 Samuel 11:1-27; 12:1-15

In this difficult chapter of David's life, we see a moment of moral failure that would have lasting consequences. David, now established as king and enjoying peace in the land, stayed behind in Jerusalem during the spring when kings traditionally went to battle. One evening, while walking on the roof of his palace, David saw Bathsheba, the wife of Uriah, a faithful soldier in David's army, bathing. He was struck by her beauty and despite being a king, with the power to take whatever he wanted, David allowed his desires to overrule his integrity.

Bathsheba soon discovered she was pregnant, and David, trying to cover up his sin, called Uriah back from the battlefield, hoping he would sleep with his wife and think the child was his. However, Uriah, showing great loyalty to his comrades in arms, refused to enjoy the comforts of home while his fellow soldiers were still fighting. David's attempt to cover up the sin failed, and his desperation led him to a more heinous act: he sent Uriah to the front lines of battle, where he would be killed.

After Uriah's death, David took Bathsheba as his wife. At first, it seemed that David had gotten away with his sin, but God saw what David had done, and He sent the prophet Nathan to confront him. Nathan told David a parable about a rich man who took a poor man's beloved lamb to feed a traveller, and David, angered by the injustice in the story, declared that the rich man deserved to die. Nathan, in turn, told David, "You are the man!"

The confrontation broke David's heart, and he immediately recognised the gravity of his sin. Nathan informed David that, although God had forgiven him, there would be consequences: the child born of Bathsheba would die, and David's household would experience turmoil as a result of his actions. David's response was one of deep repentance, and he acknowledged his sin before God, saying, "*I have sinned against the Lord*" (2 Samuel 12:13).

David's repentance was sincere, but the consequences were severe. The child born to Bathsheba did indeed die, but later, God gave David and Bathsheba another son, **Solomon**, who would go on to become king and build the temple that David had longed to build.

Reflection

This is one of the most difficult stories in David's life, showing that even a man after God's own heart is not immune to sin. David's fall reminds us that no one is beyond temptation and that even those with a heart for God can make grave mistakes. David's actions (adultery, deception, and murder) were not small sins. However, what stands out in this story is not only David's sin but also his immediate repentance when confronted by the prophet Nathan.

David's response teaches us about the **power of repentance**. When confronted with the reality of his sin, David did not make excuses or attempt to justify his actions. Instead, he humbled himself before God and acknowledged his wrongdoing. **True repentance** involves not just feeling sorrow for sin but also recognising the need for God's mercy and grace. David's heart was broken over his sin, and this was the first step in the process of healing.

God forgave David, but there were consequences for his actions. This shows Christians that while **God is merciful**, our choices have consequences. David's family would experience turmoil as a result of his sin, but God's forgiveness didn't mean the erasure of the impact his sin had on others. However, even in the midst of his failure, God was still working through David's life. God gave him a second chance, and from the relationship with Bathsheba, He gave him Solomon, through whom the line of David would continue.

David's story also shows that **God's grace is greater than our failures**. Even in the midst of his sin, God didn't abandon David, and He still had a great plan for David's life and legacy. Despite David's moral failure, he was still remembered as a man after God's own heart, because he **repented** and sought forgiveness.

From a neutral perspective:

David's sin with Bathsheba stands as a stark reminder that even the greatest of men fall when desire overcomes duty. His power allowed him to take, but it could not shield him from the weight of guilt or the reach of justice. The consequences (broken trust, family strife, and divine chastisement) reveal that no one, not even a king, is beyond accountability. Yet, in his repentance, David shows that true greatness is not in being faultless but in seeking redemption. His story reminds us that while our choices shape our fate, grace remains for those who turn back with a contrite heart.

A Sister's Light

"Repentance isn't just about asking for forgiveness; it is about understanding the weight of our mistakes and what we do after that truly matters. Repentance is the key to moving forward and this starts with a humble heart."

Journalling Invitations

1. **David's sin with Bathsheba shows that even those who are close to God can make serious mistakes.**

Reflect on a time when you experienced personal failure or a moral struggle. How did you respond in that moment?

How can you learn to face your mistakes with humility and a willingness to grow, knowing that self-compassion and the opportunity for renewal are always within reach?

2. **David's repentance was sincere, and he acknowledged his sin before God.**

When you've made a mistake or fallen short of your own values, do you find yourself justifying your actions or trying to hide them? How can you approach yourself with honesty and humility, seeking growth, healing, and a renewed sense of integrity?

3. **God forgave David, but there were still consequences for his actions.**

Are there areas in your life where your choices have had lasting consequences on others? How have you worked to restore those relationships or make amends?

What steps can you take to repair the damage caused by your actions?

4. **God's forgiveness didn't erase the pain caused by David's sin, but it gave him a chance to move forward.**

Is there something in your life that you need to move forward from, even though the consequences are still present?

How can you trust that your story still holds the potential for healing, growth, and beauty, even while it feels so broken?

5. **Despite his failure, God continued to work through David's life.**

Christians: How can you recognise God's continued work in your life, even when you feel undeserving of His grace?

What ways can you continue to surrender to God's purposes, knowing that He can use even our failures for His glory?

David's sin with Bathsheba is a sobering reminder that even the most faithful followers of God can fall into temptation. However, for Christians, David's story also demonstrates the **power of repentance** and **God's incredible grace**. No matter how great our failures, God is always ready to forgive and restore us when we approach Him with a humble and contrite heart.

David's Grief over his Child's Death

2 Samuel 12:15-23

After David's sin with Bathsheba and his repentance, God had promised to forgive him, but the consequences of his actions would still unfold. The child born to David and Bathsheba became seriously ill, and David prayed earnestly for the child's life. He fasted, wept, and lay on the ground, refusing to eat, hoping that God would show mercy and spare his child.

His servants were deeply concerned, seeing how broken David was, but they were afraid to tell him the truth once the child passed, fearing his grief would be unbearable. When David saw them whispering, he realised that his son had died. Instead of responding with anger or bitterness, David got up, washed, anointed himself, changed his clothes, and went to the house of the Lord to worship.

He then returned to his palace and began to eat. His servants were confused by his behaviour, as it seemed strange that he would stop mourning after the death of his child. But David explained, *"While the child was still alive, I fasted and wept. I thought, 'Who knows? The Lord may be gracious to me and let the child live.' But now that he is dead, why should I fast? Can I bring him back again? I will go to him, but he will not return to me"* (2 Samuel 12:22-23).

David's response to the death of his child shows his understanding of God's will, even in the face of deep sorrow. He accepted the outcome with a sense of peace, knowing that his grief, while profound, could not change what had happened. His worship and trust in God during this time showed that, even in his grief, his faith remained steadfast.

Reflection

David's mourning and his response to his child's death teach us something powerful about how to process grief and loss. Grief is a deeply personal journey, and it takes time to heal. David's actions were not an attempt to deny his sorrow but rather an expression of submission to God's will. He understood that God's plan was beyond his understanding and that sometimes, the only thing to do in the midst of sorrow is to trust God and continue forward in faith.

David's journey through grief is a reminder that God is present in our pain, and while we may not always understand why certain things happen, God is faithful to walk with us through our darkest times. His willingness to worship God in the midst of tragedy shows that even in the hardest of circumstances, God is worthy of our praise.

David's faith is a testament to the fact that grief doesn't have to lead to despair. It can lead to peace and trust in God's eternal love. David knew that while he could not change the past, he could keep his eyes on the future and the hope of being reunited with his son.

A Reflection on David's Grief

When David's child falls ill, we see him in raw, anguished prayer — fasting, weeping, lying on the ground. He pleads with God for mercy, for healing, for a different outcome. But when the child dies, something unexpected happens: David rises. He bathes, changes his clothes, worships, and eats.

It is a scene that startles the onlookers, even his servants. But David, in his quiet wisdom, offers a deeply human and spiritual truth: *"Can I bring him back again? I shall go to him, but he shall not return to me."*

In these few words, David does not deny his grief. He does not explain it away or pretend it never happened. Rather, he accepts what is painful and irreversible, and finds the strength to move forward. His faith allows him to look beyond the grave, to a reunion that will come in God's time.

David's response is not about stoicism, but surrender. Not about forgetting, but remembering with hope. In grief, he teaches us not to fight what we cannot change, but to live with reverence for what was, and with trust in what will be.

His story reminds us that faith does not shield us from loss—it guides us through it.

A Sister's Light

"When grief comes, it's okay to cry and mourn. But grief doesn't have to hold us hostage. As we mourn, we can also find peace, knowing that God/the Divine is with us even when we don't have all the answers. Trust God's love is big enough to carry us through our hardest days."

Journalling Invitations

1. **David's grief was real and raw, but he turned to God in worship even in his sorrow.**
How do you typically respond to grief or difficult circumstances?
Do you turn to God for comfort and strength, or do you tend to withdraw during times of pain?

2. **David recognised that his child could not come back to him, but he would one day go to him.**
What does this statement reveal about David's understanding of life and death?
How can this perspective help you when you experience loss or when facing things beyond your control?

3. **David accepted the death of his child with peace, knowing that he couldn't change the outcome.**
Are there situations in your life where you are holding on to something that is beyond your control?
How can you begin to release your grip on it and trust God's will, even when you don't understand the outcome?

4. **The journey through grief is a personal one, but David's actions demonstrate the power of worship in the midst of sorrow.**
How can worship, prayer, or other spiritual practices help you in times of loss or sadness?

5. David didn't deny his sorrow, but he also didn't allow it to consume him.

How do you balance acknowledging your grief while also maintaining hope?

In what ways can you allow **hope** to rise alongside your grief, knowing that God is with you in both?

David's grief over his child's death is a moving example of how **faith** and **trust** can coexist with deep sorrow. He mourned, but he also accepted the reality of his situation and continued to worship God. His story reminds us that grief does not have to lead us into despair, but can instead be the **beginning of healing**, as we trust God with our pain.

A prayer for those who grieve:

Dear Lord,
When sorrow visits and my heart feels heavy, help me to remember that You are near.
In the stillness after loss, when words fall away, fill the silence with Your peace.
I know grief is not a sign of weakness; it is love with no place to go.
But even in the ache, I trust You.
Even in the letting go, I lean into Your promise.
Thank You for the time we are given, for every breath, every smile, every tear.
And when it is time to say goodbye on this side of Heaven, remind my loved ones that we are never truly apart ...
only waiting, only trusting, only one sunrise closer to reunion.
Until then, I will live with joy,
love without holding back,
and rest in Your eternal embrace.
Amen."

Let's continue with **David's story** — the **rebellion of his son Absalom** and the emotional and spiritual toll it took on David. This chapter explores **fatherhood, betrayal**, and **God's sovereignty** in the midst of great personal turmoil.

Absalom: The Wounded Son ... the story retold

Absalom was David's son; a prince known for his striking beauty, charisma, and deep love for his sister, Tamar. When their half-brother Amnon violated Tamar and David failed to act justly, a seed of anger and sorrow took root in Absalom's heart. He waited two years before taking justice into his own hands, ordering the death of Amnon. Afterward, Absalom fled into exile.

Though David longed to see him, he did not reach out. Years passed in silence before Absalom was finally allowed to return to Jerusalem but even then, he did not see his father's face for two more years. The distance between them grew.

Eventually, Absalom's pain hardened into rebellion. He stole the hearts of the people and declared himself king. David, once again heartbroken, fled from Jerusalem. In the end, Absalom was killed in battle despite David's command to spare his life.

When news of his son's death reached David, he was undone. He wept bitterly: *"O my son Absalom, my son, my son Absalom! Would I had died instead of you — O Absalom, my son, my son!"*

A Reflection

This is a story of heartbreak that unfolds in slow motion; a grief that begins long before death, through silence, distance, and misunderstanding.

David failed to defend Tamar, and Absalom could not understand his father's inaction. In trying to take justice into his own hands, Absalom became caught in a spiral of bitterness, perhaps hoping that each act of defiance would finally claim his father's attention, his remorse, his love.

But neither spoke the words the other most needed to hear.

By the time David reached for reconciliation, it was too late. The tragedy of Absalom is not only his rebellion or his death—it is the love that was there but unspoken, the pain that was shared but never healed.

How many relationships are marked by this same ache? Wounded hearts waiting for the other to move, say something, make it right. Absalom reminds us how crucial it is to speak of our love while we still can, to face pain with honesty, and to seek peace before it slips beyond our grasp.

A Prayer for those who are hurting...

Lord of Mercy,
You see what lies beneath our silences.
You know the words we're afraid to say,
and the love we hold back out of pride or pain.
If I could speak into the moments that were lost,
I would say: love is worth the risk.
Even when it hurts,
even when it's not returned as we hope ...
it is never wasted when it is given.
Help us forgive what was broken.
Heal the stories we carry in pieces.
And teach us to be brave enough
to reach out before the moment passes.
Amen.

Journaling Invitations

1. **Is there someone in your life with whom there is distance or silence?** What might need to be spoken or offered to begin a path toward healing?

2. **Reflect on a time when you waited for someone to make the first move.** What held you back from reaching out yourself?

3. **Write a letter (you may or may not send it)** to someone with whom things were left unresolved. What would you want them to know?

4. **How do you define justice and mercy?** Where do you see the need to balance the two in your own life or in a past experience?

Absalom's Rebellion and David's Flight

2 Samuel 15:1-30

The rebellion of **Absalom**, David's son, is one of the most painful chapters in David's life. Absalom, who had been deeply hurt by the way David handled the situation with his half-brother **Amnon** (who had raped his sister **Tamar**), began to harbour resentment against his father. Over time, Absalom used his charm and popularity to win the hearts of the people of Israel, eventually leading a conspiracy to overthrow David as king.

Absalom's rebellion was a **personal betrayal** that went beyond politics; it was an act of **family disloyalty**, and it devastated David. Absalom's supporters grew in number, and David, realising the threat, fled Jerusalem with his closest followers. As David made his way out of the city, he was met with mockery and rejection, including the curse of **Shimei**, a relative of King Saul, who blamed David for the downfall of Saul's house.

In the middle of this overwhelming situation, David's emotions were torn. He had to flee the city that had been the capital of his reign, leaving behind his throne and his home. His heart was heavy with grief, both for the rebellion of his son and the loss of his kingdom. David's flight symbolised a moment of humiliation, and it forced him to trust completely in God's will for the future.

Reflection

Absalom's rebellion is one of the most heart-wrenching events in David's life. The pain of losing his kingdom and being **betrayed by his son** was profound. This event reveals the **fragility of human relationships** and the deep **emotional toll** that comes with family conflict and betrayal. Yet, it also highlights how David, despite his grief, continued to trust in God's sovereignty.

David had to wrestle with the tension between his **love for his son** and the reality that Absalom's rebellion was tearing apart the very kingdom that David had worked so hard to establish. The hurt and emotional turmoil that David experienced reminds us that **even when we face trials**, whether from family, friends, or circumstances, God is still present, still sovereign, and still working out His plan for our lives.

David's trust in God is evident throughout this painful chapter. Although his heart was broken and his position as king was threatened, David did not take matters into his own hands with vengeance. Instead, he continued to seek God's guidance and wisdom, even in the midst of personal betrayal and public humiliation.

In our own lives, Christians can learn from David's example to submit our hearts and plans to God, even in moments of deep pain and betrayal. Trusting in God's sovereignty allows us to find peace, even in the storm. We may not always understand why things happen as they do, but we can trust that God is still in control, and He will lead us through difficult times.

The story of Absalom's rebellion and David's flight can offer spiritual reflection approached from the lens of human emotion, inner conflict, and the complexity of relationships.

In this chapter of David's life, we see a tragic breakdown of family trust and loyalty, something that resonates deeply in the human experience. Absalom, David's son, is driven by ambition, pride, and a desire for power, while David is caught in a painful struggle between his duty as king and his love for his son. This tragic rift echoes the tension many face between personal desires and their deeper moral compass.

From a spiritual perspective, this story may serve as a reminder of the importance of humility and wisdom in our own pursuits. Absalom's hunger for power, and David's reluctant flight, highlight the dangers of ego and the way it can lead individuals to distance themselves from their true purpose or calling. David's sorrowful retreat, though it might be seen as a defeat, also exemplifies a quiet strength: the wisdom to let go and allow for the course of events to unfold, rather than trying to control or force an outcome. There is power in surrender and acceptance; recognising that some battles, especially those involving deep relationship wounds, cannot be fought with force or pride but need space for healing.

On a personal level, this story may prompt reflection on the relationships in our own lives. Are there moments when our desires or pride have caused rifts, either within ourselves or with those we care about? The challenge here is to understand when to stand firm and when to step back in humility, recognising that sometimes, the act of stepping back can be the greatest form of strength.

The narrative also explores the concept of exile, not just in a physical sense but also in a spiritual sense. David's flight symbolises the feeling of being separated from one's sense of security, identity, and purpose. This kind of spiritual exile often emerges during times of conflict, change, or betrayal, and can lead to deep introspection. Yet, it is in these moments of vulnerability that one can also experience profound growth and clarity, as David did through his journey.

In reflecting on this story, we might ask ourselves: How do we respond to conflict or betrayal? Do we react with anger and a desire for retribution, or do we seek a more measured, peaceful resolution? Can we find strength in humility and surrender when facing overwhelming challenges?

A Sister's Light

"Sometimes, walking away from a battle is not a sign of defeat, but of wisdom and trust in the unfolding patterns of our life."

Journalling Invitations

1. **David was deeply betrayed by his son Absalom, and the rebellion tore at his heart.**
Have you ever experienced betrayal, especially from someone you loved or trusted? How did that betrayal affect you emotionally and spiritually?
How can you find healing in trusting God's plan for

your life, even when relationships are broken or painful?

2.   David's flight from Jerusalem symbolises the loss of his kingdom and his humility in the face of conflict.

Are there areas in your life where you have faced loss or humiliation? How have you responded to those moments?

How can you surrender those painful moments to God, trusting that He is working even in the midst of your struggles?

3.   David continued to trust in God's sovereignty, even though he didn't understand why his son turned against him.

In moments when life feels uncertain or when you face betrayal, how can lean into trust, even when the path forward is unclear?

4.   David was mocked and cursed by Shimei, but he didn't retaliate.

When you are falsely accused or mistreated, how do you respond? Do you seek revenge, or do you trust justice will be done?

What can you learn from David's example of humility and restraint when facing unjust treatment?

5.   David's grief over his son's rebellion was deep, but he did not let it consume him.

Are there areas in your life where grief or loss are trying to overshadow your faith in God? How can you find healing in God's presence during your grief?

How can you focus on trusting God's greater purpose, even when life is filled with emotional turmoil?

David's experience of **Absalom's rebellion** reminds us that even the most beloved leaders and faithful followers of God can experience profound **betrayal** and **loss**. Yet, David's response shows us how to handle such crises with **humility**,

faith, and a continued trust in **God's sovereignty**. Even in the depths of grief, God was still working through David's life.

The Death of Absalom

2 Samuel 18:1-33

After Absalom's rebellion against David, there was a final confrontation between Absalom's army and David's forces. David's heart was torn, knowing that this battle would likely cost the life of his beloved son. Despite the overwhelming odds, David instructed his commanders to deal gently with Absalom for his sake, saying, *"Be gentle with the young man Absalom for my sake"* (2 Samuel 18:5). His love for Absalom, despite the rebellion, was clear: David's heart still ached for his son.

The battle ended in victory for David, but it came with devastating news. **Absalom was killed** in the battle after his long hair got caught in a tree, leaving him hanging helplessly. One of David's commanders, **Joab**, took matters into his own hands and killed Absalom, even though David had specifically asked for him to be spared.

When the news reached David, his joy over the victory turned into overwhelming sorrow. The grief he experienced at the death of his son was profound. He cried out in anguish, *"O my son Absalom, my son, my son Absalom! If only I had died instead of you, O Absalom, my son, my son!"* (2 Samuel 18:33). David's words reflect the deep, **unbearable pain** a parent feels when they lose a child, whether through rebellion, death, or estrangement.

The loss of Absalom was a deeply emotional moment in David's life, and it affected the entire kingdom. David's men, who had fought for him, saw his reaction and wondered if David still cared for them, considering his overwhelming sorrow for his son's death. Despite their victory, David's grief overshadowed the moment, and he needed to be reminded of the loyalty and sacrifices of his men.

Reflection

The death of Absalom is a tragic culmination of the deep emotional and relationship turmoil that David had been enduring. On one hand, David had been **vindicated** in battle, but on the other, his son's **death** left him in **profound**

sorrow. David's reaction teaches us that even in the midst of great personal **victory**, loss and grief can still overshadow our hearts, especially when they involve **family**.

David's deep mourning for Absalom highlights the **unconditional love** he had for his son, despite Absalom's rebellion. It also reflects the complex nature of **human relationships**. Even though Absalom had tried to take David's throne, David's heart could not let go of the love he had for his son. In a way, this moment reveals David's **struggle between justice and love** ... a parent's deep longing for reconciliation, even when their child has chosen a path of destruction.

David's **grief** also shows us the **importance of mourning**. We see that it is okay to mourn, even deeply, when we face loss, and that grief is a natural part of the healing process. However, it's also a reminder that we must find a way to move forward, to acknowledge the **loyalty** and **sacrifices of others**, and to honour the victories that have been achieved.

In our own lives, when we face loss, whether through **death**, **estrangement**, or **betrayal**, Christians are called to bring their grief before God. **God understands our pain** and invites us to grieve in His presence. However, we are also called to look beyond our sorrow to **move forward in faith**, trusting that God/the Divine can bring **healing** and **redemption**, even from the deepest wounds.

A Sister's Light

"Grief is a heavy companion to carry but we don't have to carry it alone. God walks beside us in those painful times, helping us to heal and guiding us forward even when it feels impossible. Grief might change us but it doesn't have to define us."

Journalling Invitations

1. **David's grief for Absalom was deeply personal, despite the rebellion.**
Have you experienced the loss of a loved one or a relationship, where the grief seemed almost unbearable?
How did you process that grief, and how did you find solace in God's/the Divine's presence during that time?

2. **David's reaction to Absalom's death shows the depth of a parent's love, even when their child has hurt them.**
Have you ever had to come to terms with the actions of someone you love, especially when they have hurt or betrayed you?
How can you find peace and healing in those situations, while still holding on to the love you have for them?

3. **The men who had fought for David saw his mourning and wondered if he cared for them.**
Sometimes we experience deep sorrow that may affect the way others see us. How do you balance personal mourning with being present for those who depend on you?
How can you show appreciation for those who have supported you, even when your grief is consuming?

4. **David's grief did not change the reality of the situation, but he needed to move forward.**
When you are going through painful times, how do you find the strength to keep moving forward?
Are there ways you can acknowledge the victories in your life, even while feeling the weight of your losses?

5. **David's mourning was not just a moment of sadness, but a moment to reflect on his son and their relationship.**
How can you use moments of loss to reflect on the

relationships in your life?
What can you learn about yourself and others through the lens of grief and reconciliation?

David's response to **Absalom's death** highlights the complexities of **love, betrayal, loss**, and **forgiveness**. Even in his most painful moments, David demonstrated a love for his son that transcended all of Absalom's rebellion. As we face our own moments of grief and loss, may we remember that **God's presence** is with us, and that **He is working** even through our deepest sorrow to bring healing and restoration.

Let's continue with the next chapter in **David's life**, focusing on **David's sin with the census** and the consequences that followed. This chapter highlights the theme of **pride, self-reliance**, and the **importance of repentance** in the face of sin.

☽✦ Handwritten Reflections ✦☽

You are invited to sit quietly with what you've read. Below is space for your own thoughts, prayers, or dreams that rise as you ponder these bible stories and their meaning in your life.

✎

✎

✎

✎

✎

✎

✎

❋ *"The heavens declare the glory of God; the skies proclaim the work of His hands." —* Psalm 19:1 ❋
Let these pages be your sacred sky.

David's Sin with the Census and its Consequences

2 Samuel 24:1-25
1 Chronicles 21:1-30

At the height of his reign, David took a census of Israel, counting the number of fighting men in his kingdom. While this may seem like a strategic move for organising his military, it was actually an act of pride and self-reliance. Instead of trusting in God's strength and provision, David was placing his confidence in the size of his army.

The decision to take the census was provoked by Satan, who incited David to count the people, which led to a direct violation of God's command to trust in Him alone for protection and victory. Joab, David's commander, tried to dissuade him, warning that the act was sinful, but David insisted.

After the census was taken, God was displeased with David's pride and lack of faith. As a result, **God sent the prophet Gad** to deliver a message of judgement, offering David three choices for the punishment:

1. Three years of famine in the land.
2. Three months of fleeing from enemies.
3. Three days of plague in the land.

David, acknowledging his sin, chose the plague, saying, *"Let us fall into the hands of the Lord, for His mercy is great; but do not let me fall into human hands"* (2 Samuel 24:14). God sent a plague that killed 70,000 people.

After the devastation, **David prayed** for the people, acknowledging that he alone was responsible for their suffering. God responded by sending an angel to stop the plague. The angel stopped at a threshing floor owned by **Araunah the Jebusite**, where David built an altar and offered sacrifices to God. God accepted the sacrifice, and the plague was averted.

Reflection

David's sin in counting the people reveals the dangerous temptation of **pride** and **self-reliance**. At the peak of his success, he forgot that it was God who had given him victory, not the number of soldiers at his command. Instead of relying on God's strength, David was drawn into the trap of measuring his own power and security by worldly standards.

The consequences of David's sin were grave, resulting in the loss of life. Yet, David's **repentance** was immediate and genuine. He took full responsibility for the people's suffering and called out for God's mercy. In his humility, he chose to trust God's judgement, showing that he understood the weight of his actions.

I want to spend a little more time on this story because I know I am not alone in feeling disturbed by this. The account of David's census (and the tragic aftermath) is one of the most difficult and mysterious episodes in Scripture. It is found in 2 Samuel 24 and also in 1 Chronicles 21, and it raises deep questions about justice, leadership, and divine judgement.

Reading this with a heart of compassion and respect for the sacredness of human life, it can be hard to understand.

Wrestling with the Harshness

It is natural and even necessary to wrestle with this passage. Seventy thousand lives lost; seemingly because of a leader's pride! This challenges our sense of fairness. It can seem as if people are being punished for something they did not choose.

Many spiritual thinkers have wrestled with this story and offered possible ways of understanding it. Here are a few lenses through which you might reflect:

The Weight of Leadership and Interconnectedness

In ancient Israel, the king was seen as a spiritual representative of the people. When David sinned, especially in a public, national act like a census (which may have reflected pride, military ambition, or lack of trust in God), the entire nation was affected. We see this today too — leaders' decisions often have far-reaching consequences on the lives of ordinary people.

Spiritually, this can be seen as a warning about the gravity of leadership, and a reminder of how interconnected we are.

Injustice or sin at the top can trickle down in devastating ways. That truth, painful as it is, reminds us to pray for leaders and hold them accountable.

A Consequence ... Not a Punishment

Some interpreters view this not as God angrily punishing people, but as the lifting of God's protective hand from a nation that had already drifted toward pride or self-sufficiency. David's act may have revealed or mirrored a wider spiritual malaise in the land. The plague, then, is not so much a wrathful punishment as a natural and painful consequence of collective spiritual choices.

Even within this dark moment, God's mercy is present. David sees the angel of death approaching Jerusalem and begs God to spare the people: *"I alone have sinned and done wrong. Let your hand fall on me and my family."* In response, God stops the plague. At the very place where the angel stops, David builds an altar — and that site becomes the future location of the Temple. Out of devastation comes a sacred new beginning.

This reminds us that God can bring healing and hope even out of our worst failures. The story does not end in destruction, but in worship and redemption.

Reading Through the Lens of Christ

From a Christian perspective, it's important to remember that Jesus reveals God's full heart: compassionate, self-sacrificing, and always close to the suffering. When we read the Old Testament through the lens of Christ, we see that God's ultimate desire is not destruction, but mercy.

The story of David's census may reflect a culture that saw suffering and divine judgement differently than we do. But Jesus, the Son of David, shows us a deeper truth: God does not desire the death of any person, but rather that all come to life and healing.

So, this story is hard for us to understand. Seventy thousand lives lost over one man's decision? It is natural, even faithful, to ask: How could a loving God allow such suffering?

Scripture does not shy away from stories that disturb us. Instead, it invites us to sit with them, to wrestle and wonder and pray. Perhaps the people were not punished so much as they were caught in the consequences of a king's pride; much like how nations today bear the wounds of power misused.

David's sin was not in counting people, but in forgetting whose people they were. The census was an act of control, a tally of might, a moment of prideful independence. His failure reminds us how easily human hearts — especially in positions of leadership — can drift from trust in God to trust in numbers, strength, or self.

And yet ... God's mercy breaks through. The plague stops. David builds an altar. The place of death becomes the place of future worship. In the ruins of brokenness, a seed of redemption is planted.

In our own lives, we may carry grief for things we cannot make sense of — moments where innocent people suffer, or where we see the cost of mistakes ripple far and wide. God does not dismiss these sorrows. In Christ, we see a God who enters into suffering, who walks among the broken-hearted, and who transforms places of pain into sacred ground.

Sometimes the questions will linger. But even in the darkest valleys, God is still a God of mercy. The altar still stands.

A Tender Closing Thought

It's okay to bring your sorrow and confusion to God. The psalms (many of which David himself wrote) are full of questions and laments. God is not offended by your honesty; in fact, it's an act of faith to ask, "How can this be just?"

A Sister's Light

" Let your heart remain open, even when understanding is hard. Sometimes, the deepest spiritual growth happens not when we resolve every mystery, but when we learn to trust that love and justice still prevail; even during the hard questions."

Journalling Invitations

1.   David's pride led him to rely on his own strength rather than God's.
Do you find it easy or difficult to rely on God during times of success or abundance?
How can you remind yourself to trust God in moments when things are going well?

2.   David repented and took responsibility for his sin, asking for God's mercy.
How do you handle moments when you realise you've made a mistake or misstep?
What does **genuine repentance** look like for you?

3.   David chose the plague, trusting God's mercy over human judgement.
How do you react when faced with consequences for your actions?
Are you able to trust God's mercy, even when the consequences are hard?

4.   The people suffered due to David's sin, but David's repentance brought an end to the plague.
Are there areas in your life where your actions may be affecting others?
How can you make things right with others when your choices have hurt them?

5.   David built an altar to God, acknowledging His sovereignty and seeking His forgiveness.
What does **worship** look like in your life, especially after moments of failure or sin?
How can worship be an expression of both repentance and gratitude for God's mercy?

Additional Journaling Invitations

What feelings does this story stir in you ...confusion, anger, sorrow, compassion? Write honestly.

Have you ever seen the consequences of a leader's choices affect the many? How did it shape your view of justice or God/the Divine?

Where in your own life have you seen pain transformed into something sacred—where loss gave way to grace?

What would your own "altar" look like ... a place where you met God in the ruins and began again?

David's story in this chapter teaches us about the dangers of **pride** and the **importance of humility**. It also reminds us that **God's mercy** is available to us when we repent and turn back to Him. **Self-reliance** may lead to sin, but **humility** and **trust** in God's grace bring restoration. David's response to his sin and his plea for God's mercy show us the path to healing and reconciliation with God, no matter how far we may have fallen.

David's story is filled with many important moments and life/spiritual lessons. Let's continue with another key chapter in his life ... **David's final instructions to Solomon**. This chapter marks the closing of David's life and his passing of the baton to Solomon, his son, to lead the people of Israel.

David's Final Instructions to Solomon

1 Kings 2:1-12

As David's life drew to a close, he gathered Solomon, his son and successor, and shared some final words of wisdom and guidance. These instructions were meant to prepare Solomon for the weight of kingship and to ensure that he would remain faithful to God throughout his reign.

David's advice was both practical and spiritual. He urged Solomon to **be strong**, **act like a man**, and follow the **ways of the Lord** with **integrity** and **faithfulness**. David emphasised the importance of keeping God's commandments, for in doing so, Solomon would prosper and fulfil the promise that God had made to David ...that his descendants would rule Israel forever.

David also reminded Solomon to be just and **fair in his leadership**. He mentioned some unfinished business that Solomon would need to address, such as dealing with certain individuals who had opposed David's rule. These matters were to be handled with wisdom, and David trusted that Solomon, under God's guidance, would have the strength to make the right decisions.

Finally, David **blessed Solomon** and passed on the throne to him, recognising that it was not his own power that had allowed him to rule, but God's favour and grace. As David passed on the reigns to Solomon, he reminded him that it was God's plan for him to continue the legacy of Israel's kingship.

Reflection

David's final words to Solomon serve as a **legacy of faith** and **leadership**. His instructions were not only about political power but about **spiritual integrity**. David understood that true success in life came from following God, and he passed this wisdom on to his son.

David's concern for Solomon's well-being wasn't just about ensuring that he was prepared to lead the people of Israel; it was about ensuring that Solomon would remain faithful to God. David's own life had been marked by moments of great

faith and moments of great **failure**, but in the end, he placed his hope in God's covenant promises.

As Solomon stepped into his role as king, David's instructions were a reminder that leadership (whether in a kingdom, a family, or in any area of life) requires a foundation of **faithfulness** to God, to others. David knew that the success of Solomon's reign depended on the strength and wisdom that came from obeying God and walking in His ways.

David's final words also show us the importance of **preparing others** for their own journeys. David didn't hold onto his power for selfish reasons; instead, he made sure that Solomon understood what was required to live a life of integrity and to fulfil God's plan. It is a reminder that, whether in leadership or relationships, we are called to **invest in others** and **empower them** to fulfil their own God-given purpose or to reach their true potential.

A Sister's Light

"The most meaningful gift we can offer others ... whether children, friends, or those we guide ... is the wisdom to live with integrity, purpose, and compassion. True leadership begins with inner alignment, and the greatest gift we can make to those we love is to walk alongside them in truth, encouraging a life rooted in what is good, just, and enduring."

Journalling Invitations

1.   **David's instructions to Solomon were filled with wisdom and concern for his faithfulness to God.**

How do you pass on wisdom and guidance to those you care about?

In what ways can you emphasise the importance of faith and integrity in your relationships?

2.   **David emphasised the importance of leadership that is rooted in obedience to God.**

What does leadership look like in your life?

How can you ensure that your leadership is guided by God's principles, not just your own strength or wisdom?

3. **David's legacy wasn't just about power but about faithfulness to God.**

When you think of the legacy you want to leave, what values do you want to pass on to others?

How can you live today in a way that reflects the values you want to leave behind?

4. **David's final words to Solomon were both practical and spiritual.**

How do you balance **practical wisdom** and **spiritual guidance** in your life?

How can you encourage others to seek both in their own journeys?

5. **David's concern for Solomon was that he would remain faithful to God.**

How do you ensure that your relationship with God remains the foundation of your life, especially in times of transition or change?

How can you help others stay grounded in faith during challenging times?

David's story is a one of faith, leadership, and legacy. His final instructions to Solomon remind us that true **leadership** and **success** come from **faithfulness to God** and **humility**. As we reflect on David's life and his desire for Solomon to walk in God's ways, we are called to examine our own relationships and leadership, ensuring that our actions are always rooted in God's wisdom and truth.

David's Final Words and Death

1 Kings 2:10-12
1 Chronicles 29:26-30

After David gave his final instructions to Solomon, he passed away and was **buried in the City of David**, marking the end of his reign. **Solomon succeeded him as king**, and under Solomon's leadership, Israel would enter into a time of peace and prosperity.

Before his death, David's **final words** as we have just discussed, were a reflection of his life's journey, emphasising the **importance of walking in God's ways** and remaining faithful to His promises. David had lived through many victories and **failures**, and he wanted to pass on to Solomon the lesson that obedience to God was the key to true success and peace.

David's words also centred on God's faithfulness. He recognised that his reign had not been marked by his own strength but by God's grace and favour. He was deeply aware that God had chosen him to be king and had established his dynasty, which would be fulfilled through Solomon.

As David passed the throne to Solomon, he encouraged his son to **be strong** and **faithful** in his service to God. He also reminded him of the **importance of the temple**, which David had long desired to build but was told by God that his son Solomon would complete it. David's instructions were a reminder to Solomon of the covenant God had made with Israel, and how that covenant would continue through his reign.

In **1 Chronicles 29**, David's final actions before his death were not just about preparing Solomon to be king, but also about **commemorating God's goodness**. David prayed and offered a final act of worship, blessing the people and praising God for His provision in their lives. He gave generously toward the building of the temple, and his offering set an example for others to follow.

Reflection
David's final words and actions demonstrate a heart that
was **humble**, **grateful**, and **faithful** to God. He didn't view
his reign as something he had earned, but as a gift from God.
Even as he prepared to step aside and let Solomon take over,
David's focus remained on the **promise of God's
faithfulness** to his family and to Israel.

One of the most striking aspects of David's final words is his
awareness of God's sovereignty. He understood that the
success of his reign and the future of Israel were not
dependent on his own efforts but on God's **grace** and
provision. David's life was a **testimony** to God's ability to
work through imperfect people, and he wanted Solomon to
carry that understanding forward.

David's **final legacy** was one of **worship** and **obedience**.
His last act was to offer praise and worship to God for all He
had done in his life. David's life was filled with moments of
great triumphs and **great failures**, but through it all, he
remained rooted in his relationship with God.

As we reflect on David's final words, Christians are
reminded that our lives are not about accumulating power or
wealth but about **faithfulness** to God's calling. Like David,
we are called to recognise God's sovereignty, praise Him for
His goodness, and pass on a legacy of faithfulness to future
generations.

Reflections for the spiritual but non-religious: **The
Measure of a Life**
At the end of a long and interesting life, David's final words
were not about battles won or titles held, but about the weight
of integrity, the pursuit of justice, and the power of living in
alignment with something greater than oneself. His journey
was far from perfect, yet in his final breath, there was clarity:
that a life of meaning is not defined by perfection, but by the
courage to seek wisdom, to learn, to grow.

In our own lives, as we move through seasons of change, we
might ask ourselves: What legacy are we leaving behind? Have
we lived with trust, with honesty, with purpose? In the quiet
closing of a chapter, there is an invitation ... not to regret what

has passed, but to honour it, and to live the remaining days with intention and grace.

A Sister's Light
"Our legacies are shaped by what we nurture in others ... especially when we help them connect with their inner truth, purpose, and the greater good."

Journalling Invitations

1. **David's final words to Solomon were about walking in God's ways and remaining faithful.**
What are the key values you want to pass on to others, especially those who will carry on after you?
How can you begin investing in future generations now?

2. **David acknowledged that his reign was not about his own strength but about God's favour.**
In your life, how do you recognise and acknowledge God's sovereignty and grace in your achievements?
What are some ways you can express gratitude for God's/Divine's provision?

3. **David's final actions were about giving generously to the temple and offering worship to God.**
How do you express worship and gratitude in your own life?
Are there areas where you can **give more generously**, not just with finances but with time, talents, and love?

4. **David's legacy was marked by his relationship with God, which he passed on to Solomon.**
What do you want your legacy to be?

How can you live today in a way that will reflect the values you want to leave behind?

5. **David's final days were filled with trust in God's promises and a desire for God's will to be done through Solomon's reign.**
How do you align your goals and desires with a deeper sense of purpose in your life? How can you trust that the right path will unfold, even amidst transitions and changes?

David's final moments reveal a heart that was focused on **obedience**, **gratitude**, and **faithfulness** to God's plan. His life and legacy remind us that it's not about what we accomplish on our own, but about how we align ourselves with God's will and pass on faith to others.

May we, like David, live with the understanding that a greater sense of purpose guides all that we do, and that our legacy is shaped by our commitment to truth and integrity.

Further contemplation ...

If you, like me, now wonder: **Do David's descendants still rule over Israe**l, I did a little research on this ...

According to the Bible, God promised King David that his descendants would reign forever (2 Samuel 7:12–16). This promise (sometimes called the *Davidic Covenant*) has been cherished by both Jewish and Christian traditions.

Historically, David's royal line continued through his son Solomon and several generations of kings in the ancient Kingdom of Judah. However, the monarchy ended when the Babylonians conquered Jerusalem around 586 BCE, destroyed the Temple, and took many Israelites into exile. From that point, no Davidic king ruled Israel in a political or national sense.

Today, modern Israel is a democratic republic, not a monarchy, so there is no reigning royal family. However, many Jewish families believe they are descended from David, and in Jewish tradition, the expected Messiah (*Mashiach*) is prophesied to come from David's line: a spiritual and redemptive fulfilment of that ancient promise.

In Christianity, that promise is also believed to be fulfilled in Jesus, who is described in the New Testament as being born of David's lineage (e.g., Matthew 1:1, Luke 1:32). So while David's royal descendants no longer rule Israel in a literal, governmental sense, his spiritual and symbolic legacy continues in both faith traditions.

Would you like a short reflection or journaling thought on that? It ties beautifully into hope and enduring promises.

Reflection: The Promise That Endures

David's crown may no longer rest on earthly heads, yet the promise God made to him echoes through the ages ... not as a throne of gold, but as a lineage of faith, hope, and purpose. In both Jewish and Christian hearts, his story reminds us that God's promises often transcend what we can see. What begins as a royal line becomes a spiritual legacy ... one that speaks of covenant, perseverance, and divine faithfulness. Even when earthly reigns fall, God's word stands.

Sometimes, the most lasting kingdoms are the ones built not with stone, but with trust.

)✦ *Handwritten Reflections* ✦)

You are invited to sit quietly with what you've read. Below is space for your own thoughts, prayers, or dreams that rise as you ponder these bible stories and their meaning in your life.

✎

✎

✎

✎

✎

✎

✎

✎

★ *"The heavens declare the glory of God; the skies proclaim the work of His hands."* — Psalm 19:1 ★
Let these pages be your sacred sky.

WOMEN OF THE BIBLE

These stories celebrate the unique roles of women and invite reflection on how we all can embody faithfulness in challenging times.

Story: Eve's Creation and Fall

Scripture Reference:

Genesis 2:22-23 - "Then the Lord God made a woman from the rib He had taken out of the man, and He brought her to the man. The man said, 'This is now bone of my bones and flesh of my flesh; she shall be called 'woman,' for she was taken out of man.'"

Genesis 3:6-7 - "When the woman saw that the fruit of the tree was good for food and pleasing to the eye, and also desirable for gaining wisdom, she took some and ate it. She also gave some to her husband, who was with her, and he ate it. Then the eyes of both of them were opened, and they realised they were naked; so they sewed fig leaves together and made themselves loincloths."

Eve, the first woman, was created by God to be a companion and helper to Adam, formed from his rib to symbolise unity and partnership. In the Garden of Eden, God gave them everything they needed, with one command ...to avoid eating the fruit from the tree of the knowledge of good and evil. Despite this warning, Eve was tempted by the serpent and ate the fruit, sharing it with Adam. Their disobedience led to their fall from grace, resulting in shame, separation from God, and the consequences of sin entering the world.

Reflection: The Temptation and Fall of Eve

Eve's story is a poignant reminder of the complexity of human choices. She was created in a perfect world, given everything she needed, yet she still faced temptation. The serpent deceived her, presenting the fruit as a means to gain wisdom and power, appealing to her desires. The fall happened in a moment of vulnerability ... Eve doubted God's goodness and fell for the lie that there was something better outside of God's perfect plan.

This story also shows the interconnectedness of Adam and Eve. When Eve ate the fruit, she didn't act in isolation; she shared the decision with Adam, and together, they both experienced the consequences. Their sin broke the perfect harmony they had with God, and the world would never be the same again.

The temptation Eve faced is one we all encounter in different forms, whether it's doubt, fear, or the allure of things that seem good but are not so. Eve's story challenges us to examine how we respond to temptation, reminding us that our choices have far-reaching effects, not only on ourselves but also on those around us.

A Sister's Light
"Eve's journey shows us that even in our struggles, there is always the possibility of restoration and new beginnings."

Journaling Invitations:
1. **What choices have you made that, like Eve, you later regretted?**
Reflect on a moment when you made a decision that led to consequences you didn't anticipate. How did that experience shape your relationship with God and others? Write about what you learned from that situation.

2. **How do you handle temptation in your own life?**
Eve's temptation was a moment of vulnerability. Think about the areas of your life where you face temptation. How do you guard your heart and mind against it? Journal about practical ways to stand firm in your faith during moments of trial.

3. **Consider the relationships in your life, like Eve and Adam's.**
How do your decisions affect those around you? Think

about the impact your choices (both good and bad) can have on your family, friends, or community. Write about how you can encourage and support others in making choices that align with God's will.

4.   **Eve's story is part of a bigger redemptive narrative.**

Reflect on how God's grace is present even in the midst of sin and failure. Write about how you've experienced God's redemption in your own life and how you can share this story of grace with others.

Hannah's Prayer and Samuel's Birth

1 Samuel 1:1–28

The Story

Hannah lived during a time when a woman's value was often tied to her ability to bear children. She was the beloved wife of Elkanah, yet her womb remained closed. Her rival, Peninnah, had children and made a sport of mocking Hannah's barrenness year after year, especially during their annual pilgrimage to Shiloh to offer sacrifices.

Despite Elkanah's tender love and reassurance — *"Am I not more to you than ten sons?"* — Hannah's heart remained burdened. One year, after a sacrificial meal at Shiloh, she rose and went to the temple. With bitterness of soul, she poured her heart out to the Lord, weeping and praying silently. She vowed that if God would remember her and give her a son, she would dedicate him to the Lord for all the days of his life.

Eli the priest observed her and, mistaking her silent lips for drunkenness, rebuked her. But once he understood her sorrow, he blessed her, saying, *"Go in peace, and may the God of Israel grant you what you have asked of Him."*

Hannah left with her spirit uplifted. In due time, she conceived and bore a son, whom she named Samuel, saying, *"Because I asked the Lord for him."* And when he was weaned, she brought him to the house of the Lord in Shiloh, just as she had promised. There, she left him to serve the Lord all his days.

Reflection

Hannah's story is a quiet triumph of faith, endurance, and sacrificial love. She shows us what it means to carry unspoken pain and yet entrust it to God with honesty and surrender. In a world that misjudged her (whether through

Peninnah's scorn or Eli's misunderstanding) she remained steady in her hope.

Her prayer was not just a request; it was a vow, a covenant woven from longing and love. She did not pray selfishly, but sacrificially — offering her deepest desire back to God, not knowing the outcome but trusting the One to whom she prayed.

Sometimes, like Hannah, we are asked to hold space between the ache and the answer — to live in the quiet in-between. And in that space, our prayers shape us. Hannah's story reminds us that God/the Divine hears even the silent prayers of our hearts and that something sacred is born not only in the answer but in the offering.

Inspired by my Sister's Inner Strength
"She believed in miracles not because life had been easy, but because she had whispered prayers in the dark and found strength waiting at dawn."

Journaling Invitations

1. Have you ever poured out your heart to God in a moment of deep need? What was that experience like for you?

2. Are there prayers you've prayed that have gone unanswered; or been answered differently than you expected? How do you feel about them now?

3. Hannah kept her vow and gave back the very gift she longed for. Is there something you've felt called to release or dedicate to God?

4. In what ways do you carry silent strength, like Hannah, misunderstood perhaps, but deeply faithful?

Hannah's Song of Praise

1 Samuel 2:1–10

The Story

After leaving her long-awaited son Samuel in the care of Eli the priest, Hannah did not walk away sorrowfully. Instead, her heart overflowed with praise. She lifted her voice in a prayer ... not of grief, but of rejoicing.

Her song was not just a personal thank you; it was a declaration of God's character and power. She praised the Lord as holy, a rock, and a God who knows all. She celebrated the way God lifts the lowly and humbles the proud, feeds the hungry, gives children to the barren, and raises the poor from the dust.

This was not simply a mother's joy ... it was a testimony of faith forged in trial. Hannah saw how God moves in ways the world does not expect. Strength doesn't come from status or might, but from the Lord who raises up the humble and strengthens the faithful.

Her words echo across generations as a hymn of hope ... for every woman who has waited, wept, and worshipped.

Reflection

Hannah's song is a beautiful witness to the truth that joy and pain often exist side by side. She held sorrow for years, yet when the time came to rejoice, her praise was bold, prophetic, and filled with gratitude. Her heart, once heavy with longing, had become light with trust.

Her prayer reminds us that when we speak from a place of lived experience ... when we've known what it is to be emptied and then filled again ... our praise carries a deeper resonance. It's not shallow or showy. It's real.

Hannah didn't keep her joy to herself; she let it rise and be heard. That is a kind of generosity too; sharing the grace she had received, naming God's faithfulness not only in her life but for all the lowly, all the overlooked.

In our own lives, may we remember that our story, too, might one day become a song; that the tears we shed in the quiet may water the soil of a praise yet to bloom.

Inspired by My Sister's Spirit

"She didn't wait for everything to be perfect before she sang. Her voice rose from the ashes, from the in-between, from the hope that never gave up."

Journaling Invitations

1. When have you experienced a moment of unexpected joy after a long period of waiting or hardship?

2. What would your own "song of praise" sound like today? Try writing a few lines or a short poem of gratitude.

3. Are there areas in your life where you feel God has lifted you up or strengthened you when you were weak?

4. How can you share your story of God's faithfulness with someone else who might still be waiting for their own breakthrough?

Although this part of our book is on Women of the Bible, it seems natural to look a little into Samuel's story. His is a story that offers such gentle depth ... a child learning to recognise God's voice in quiet moments just as we can still do today.

Samuel Hears God's Voice

1 Samuel 3:1–21

The Story

Samuel was still a boy when he began serving in the temple under Eli. The scripture tells us, "The word of the Lord was rare in those days; visions were not widespread." Yet something sacred stirred in the stillness.

One night, as Samuel lay down near the Ark of God, he heard someone call his name: "Samuel." Thinking it was Eli, he ran to him, saying, "Here I am!" But Eli hadn't called. This happened again — three times — before Eli realised what was happening. Gently, he told the boy, "Go and lie down, and if He calls you again, say, *'Speak, Lord, for Your servant is listening.'*"

And so it was that when the Lord called once more, Samuel responded just as Eli instructed. From that moment on, God began to reveal His word to Samuel, and the boy grew in wisdom and favour. All Israel came to know that the Lord was with him.

Reflection

There is something tender about this story ... the stillness of night, a child's innocence, and the unfamiliar sound of God's call. Samuel didn't yet know the Lord, but he knew how to respond to someone he trusted. That's how it begins for many of us: hearing through the voices and guidance of others, until one day, the voice becomes unmistakably God's own, or a recognition of your Higher Self/intuition talking to you.

It is striking that God called Samuel by name. Not once, but repeatedly. That patient persistence mirrors how God/our intuition often speaks ... not in grand pronouncements, but in repeated whispers, waiting for us to recognise His voice/our inner voice.

Samuel's posture (open, listening, willing) is the very heart of faith. "Speak, Lord, for Your servant is listening" is a prayer we can all carry with us, especially in seasons of uncertainty or change.

Even when the world is quiet or we feel small and unsure, God is not silent. He calls us by name, just as He called Samuel, with purpose and love.

A Sister's Light

"She listened for God not just in the thunder, but in the quiet ... and in that stillness, she found her calling."

Journaling Invitations

1. Have you ever felt that God was trying to get your attention? What did that feel like?

2. Who has been like Eli in your life — someone who helped you recognise the voice of God?

3. Is there a quiet invitation stirring in your heart now? What might God be whispering to you in this season?

4. Try praying or writing the simple prayer: "Speak, for I am listening." What thoughts or images come to mind?

Before returning to the Women of the Bible, let us now walk a little farther with Samuel, as he grows into the role God prepared him for ... prophet, priest, and leader. His journey offers wisdom about guidance, obedience, and listening for God's voice in every season of life.

Carole Somerville

Samuel the Prophet and Leader
1 Samuel 7:2–17 and selected verses from Chapters 8–12
The Story
As Samuel grew, the people of Israel looked to him as a spiritual leader. The Lord was with him, and his words carried weight. He became both a prophet and a judge; guiding Israel with integrity, interceding for them, and calling them back to God.

During a time of national crisis, Samuel urged the people to return to the Lord with all their hearts. They did so, putting away foreign gods and gathering at Mizpah to fast and pray. There, Samuel cried out to the Lord on their behalf, and God delivered them from their enemies. To mark the moment, Samuel raised a stone and named it *Ebenezer*, saying, "Thus far the Lord has helped us."

Yet later, the people demanded a king. Though grieved, Samuel listened to God, who told him to warn them but to give them what they asked for. Samuel obeyed; he anointed Saul as Israel's first king, remaining faithful to his calling, even when it meant letting go of his own vision for the future.

Samuel continued to pray for the people and speak the truth, always pointing them back to the Lord. His life was marked by obedience, humility, and an unwavering commitment to God's voice.

Reflection
Samuel's story invites us to consider what it means to lead with a listening heart. From the moment he first said, "Speak, Lord," Samuel became a vessel for God's guidance. He didn't seek power ... he served with faithfulness and compassion.

There is quiet strength in Samuel's leadership. He stood firm in truth, even when it was uncomfortable. He accepted God's direction, even when it meant change. He prayed for the people, even when they rejected his counsel. This is a picture of servant leadership ... not self-centred, but God-centred.

There may be moments in our own lives when we are called to stand in the middle; between what was and what will be. Like Samuel, we may not always see the fruit right away, but if we walk with integrity and keep listening for God's voice/to our inner voice, we, too, will be faithful.

The *Ebenezer stone* is a powerful symbol; a reminder that even when the road ahead is uncertain, we can look back and say with confidence, "Thus far, the Lord/the Divine has helped us."

A Sister's Light

"She never asked for recognition. She just kept walking in love, listening for God, trusting her intuition and quietly lifting others with her gentle words of wisdom."

Journaling Invitations

1. What does faithful leadership look like to you — in your family, your church, or your personal life?

2. Are there any "Ebenezers" in your life — moments you can look back on and say, "God helped me here"?

3. Has there been a time when you had to accept a change you didn't want, trusting God/the divine's direction anyway?

4. Write a prayer or reflection on what it means to say "Speak, Lord" not only in youth, but throughout life.

Now that we've completed this portion of Samuel's journey, we turn next to **Ruth.**

Ruth: Loyalty and New Beginnings

Ruth 1–4

The Story

In the days of the judges, a famine swept through Bethlehem. Elimelech, his wife Naomi, and their two sons left their home and travelled to Moab, a foreign land. There, the sons married Moabite women: Orpah and Ruth. But soon, grief shadowed their lives. First Elimelech died, and then both sons. Naomi, now widowed and heartbroken, decided to return to Bethlehem, urging her daughters-in-law to stay behind and start new lives.

Orpah kissed Naomi goodbye. But Ruth ... young, foreign, with little security ... clung to her. In one of Scripture's most moving declarations of love, Ruth said:

"Where you go, I will go.
Where you stay, I will stay.
Your people will be my people,
And your God, my God."

So together they returned to Bethlehem, where Ruth worked humbly in the fields to provide for them. She caught the eye of Boaz, a kind and honourable man who made sure she was safe and cared for. In time, through both Ruth's courage and Naomi's wisdom, Boaz redeemed Ruth, marrying her and restoring their family's line.

Their son, Obed, would become the grandfather of King David, and one day, from Ruth's lineage, the Messiah would be born.

Reflection

Ruth's story speaks of faithfulness in the face of uncertainty. She left behind all that was familiar to walk with Naomi ... not out of obligation, but out of deep love. Her journey was not grand or public, but the choices she made in quiet loyalty changed history.

We often think of courage as something loud or visible. But Ruth teaches us that some of the bravest acts are done in silence — staying when it would be easier to leave, working with dignity, trusting that grace can find us even in the fields of our ordinary days.

Ruth is also a story of second chances. Even after loss and sorrow, new life bloomed ... slowly, gently. God's providence wove through every moment, bringing redemption not just to Ruth and Naomi, but to generations to come.

In times when we feel small or unsure, Ruth reminds us that love, kindness, and faith can light the way forward. Even when we can't see the whole path, we can take the next right step.

A Sister's Light

"She followed love wherever it led, not because it was safe, but because it was right. And somehow, in that trust, she found herself home."

Journaling Invitations

1. When have you had to make a difficult decision out of love or loyalty? What did it teach you?

2. What does Ruth's quiet courage stir in you today?

3. Is there a part of your story where you've seen unexpected grace or a second beginning?

4. Try writing your own version of Ruth's vow — a statement of commitment to someone, to God, or to a new path in your life.

Esther: For Such a Time as This

Book of Esther

The Story

Esther was a young Jewish woman living in exile in Persia. With being orphaned as a child, Esther was raised by her cousin Mordecai. When the Persian king sought a new queen, Esther was chosen for her beauty but it was her wisdom and courage that would one day save a nation.

Esther kept her Jewish identity hidden at Mordecai's advice. Meanwhile, a royal official named Haman rose to power and plotted the destruction of all the Jews in the kingdom. When Mordecai learned of the decree, he urged Esther to speak to the king, a dangerous act, for no one approached the king without being summoned, not even the queen.

Esther was afraid. But she prayed, fasted, and made a choice. She said, *"I will go to the king, even though it is against the law. And if I perish, I perish."*

Esther approached the king with humility and boldness. She invited him to a banquet, then another, and at the right moment, she revealed Haman's plot and her own heritage. The king listened. Haman's plan was overturned, and the Jewish people were saved.

Esther had approached the king without being summoned, a move that could have resulted in her execution. With her bravery and wisdom, Esther saved her people and thwarted Haman's plans, making a profound impact on history.

The girl who once kept her identity hidden became the instrument of deliverance. Esther's name was forever tied to courage and divine purpose.

Reflection

Esther reminds us that courage is not the absence of fear, but the willingness to act even when fear is present. Her decision did not come easily — she prayed, waited, and stepped forward in faith.

We often find ourselves in moments we didn't ask for — seasons that stretch us, call us out, or press us to speak when silence would be easier. In those moments, Esther's story offers a guiding light. We may not see the full picture, but we can trust that we were created with intention, for such a time as this.

God was never named in Esther's story, yet His presence weaves quietly through every page ... in the timing, in the open doors, in the courage that rose within her. He works even when His name is hidden, and He often chooses the unexpected to bring about redemption.

Esther teaches us that our voice matters. Our presence matters. Even when we feel ordinary, even when we are afraid, God can use us in extraordinary ways.

Sisters ...

"Esther's legacy is one of bravery, conviction, and a deep sense of responsibility. Like a sister who steps into the gap, she shows us that sometimes, our light is revealed when we take bold action on behalf of others. Esther's light continues to shine as a symbol of the strength and influence women can have in the world. She reminds us that we too are called to rise to the occasion in times of difficulty, trusting that we are where we are for a reason.

Just as a sister might lend a listening ear or offer a comforting word, Esther demonstrates how each of us can offer courage and leadership in our own spheres of influence. Her story serves as a beacon of hope, showing us that even in the face of fear, we can choose to step into the light and make a difference."

Journaling Invitations

1. Have you ever faced a moment when you had to speak up or act with courage? What helped you find your strength?

2. Where might God/the Divine be quietly working behind the scenes in your life right now?

3. Write a letter to yourself as if you were Esther ... reminding yourself of your worth, your voice, and your purpose.

4. What does "for such a time as this" mean to you in your current season?

5. Whether it's a family member, friend, or public figure, think of a woman whose strength and faith have helped shape you. How has her example encouraged you to take brave steps in your own life? Write about her impact on you.

Deborah: A Judge and Prophet

Judges 4–5

The Story

In a time when Israel had no king, and the people often strayed from God's ways, Deborah rose as a judge — the only woman in Scripture to hold that role. She sat under a palm tree, offering wisdom and settling disputes, and the people came to her for counsel. But Deborah was more than a judge; she was also a prophet — one who listened to God and spoke with authority.

When Israel faced oppression under the cruel commander Sisera, God gave Deborah a message for Barak, a military leader: he was to gather ten thousand men and go into battle. Barak agreed — but only if Deborah would go with him.

She didn't hesitate. "I will surely go with you," she said, though she told him that the glory would not be his ... for God would deliver Sisera into the hands of a woman.

And so it was. The enemy army was defeated, and Sisera fled, only to be taken down by another courageous woman — Jael — who struck the final blow.

After the victory, Deborah sang a song of praise — a beautiful, poetic hymn recorded in Judges 5. She gave glory to God, honoured the bravery of the people, and remembered the women whose strength changed the course of history.

Reflection

Deborah's presence in Scripture is quiet but powerful. She doesn't seek attention. She listens. She leads. She encourages others to rise. Her strength comes from her closeness to God; from being rooted in truth and willing to act when called.

In many ways, Deborah's story reminds us that leadership is not about control or applause. It's about being available to God; discerning the time to speak, the time to act, and the time to sing.

Barak leaned on her strength, and she didn't shame him for it. Instead, she walked beside him, knowing that the real victory would belong to God. Her humility did not diminish her authority — it deepened it.

And even after the battle, she didn't bask in triumph. She lifted her voice in worship.

Deborah is often called "a mother in Israel," not because she had children, but because of how she led — with wisdom, nurturing strength, and fierce faith. She reminds us that we, too, can lead in whatever space we've been given, simply by being true to what God asks of us.

A Sister's Light
"She didn't need a throne or a title; just a listening heart, a steady voice, and the courage to go on when others hesitated."

Journaling Invitations
1. Where in your life are you called to be a leader, even quietly (at home, in your church, in your community)?
2. When have you seen God use your wisdom or presence to strengthen someone else?
3. What does spiritual courage look like for you today? Is there a situation where God might be calling you to "go with" someone who needs your presence?
4. Write your own short "song of victory" … a few lines of gratitude for a time when God brought you through something hard.

Next is Anna the Prophetess, a quiet but luminous figure in Scripture. Though mentioned only briefly, her life speaks volumes about devotion, faithfulness, and the joy of recognising God's promise fulfilled. Let's linger now, in her story....

Anna the Prophetess: A Life of Faithful Watching

Luke 2:36–38

The Story

Anna appears in the Gospel of Luke during a sacred moment; when Mary and Joseph bring the infant Jesus to the temple for dedication. There, in the heart of the temple courts, stands Anna: a prophetess, a widow, and a woman of deep devotion.

She is described as being "very old," having lived with her husband for only seven years before spending the rest of her long life in worship. Anna never left the temple. Day and night, she fasted, prayed, and waited ... watching for the redemption of Israel.

And then, one day, the waiting ended.

Led by the Spirit, she arrived just as Simeon held the Christ child in his arms. At that very moment, Anna gave thanks to God. She recognised the tiny baby as the fulfilment of every hope she had carried for decades. Scripture tells us she "spoke about the child to all who were looking forward to the redemption of Jerusalem."

Her moment was brief, but her faith had been long. Anna saw what many others missed ... and rejoiced.

Reflection

Anna's story is a quiet flame. She did not perform great miracles or stand before kings. Her ministry was prayer. Her offering was time. Her legacy was devotion.

In a world that often rushes past the elderly or the hidden, Anna reminds us that God honours those who wait faithfully. She shows us that spiritual strength is not always loud — sometimes, it is born of silent years, steady hope, and a heart that never gives up watching.

She had known sorrow — widowed young, likely without children, her life might have seemed lonely or overlooked. But Anna turned her grief into worship. She stayed close to the presence of God, year after year. And in doing so, she became one of the first to recognise the Messiah.

There is a quiet sanctity in those who keep the flame of faith alive through seasons of waiting. Anna's story reminds us that no moment in life is ever wasted when it is surrendered to a higher purpose. Whether we are in the prime of life or in its later years, whether our efforts are visible or not, our faithfulness holds meaning and value.

A Sister's Light
"She waited with wonder, not weariness — her hope steady as a candle's flame, lighting the way for those who came after or continue without her."

Journaling Invitations
1. Is there a prayer or hope you have held onto for a long time? What keeps your faith alive through the waiting?

2. Where have you seen God show up in quiet or unexpected ways — in "temple moments" that felt sacred?

3. Think of a person whose faith inspires you. What qualities in them remind you of Anna?

4. Write a short prayer of thanksgiving — a way of saying, "I see You, Lord," in your own life.

Huldah the Prophetess: A Voice of Truth in Sacred Places

2 Kings 22:8–20; 2 Chronicles 34:14–28

The Story

It was a time of rediscovery. King Josiah, young and earnest, sought to return his people to the ways of the Lord. In the process of repairing the temple, the high priest Hilkiah found an ancient scroll — the Book of the Law, long forgotten and covered in dust.

When the scroll was read to King Josiah, he tore his robes in grief. He realised how far the people had strayed from God's commands. But he didn't act on impulse. He wanted to understand God's will, so he sent a group of trusted men — including the priest, the scribe, and others — to seek out a prophet.

They came to Huldah.

Huldah was a prophetess living in Jerusalem, and though little is said about her background, what is clear is that she was known, respected, and trusted. When she heard the message, she spoke with divine clarity. She confirmed that the words in the scroll were true ... judgement would come for the nation's disobedience. Yet, to Josiah, she gave a word of mercy. Because of his humble heart and repentance, he would not live to see the coming calamity.

Huldah's words, though delivered quietly, outside the temple walls, shaped the reform of a nation.

Reflection

Huldah stands as a strong example of spiritual authority grounded in wisdom and humility. In a male-dominated society, she did not demand to be heard; yet when the moment came, the leaders of the land sought her out.

What gave her such credibility? Her life of faithfulness. Her alignment with truth. Her willingness to speak what was hard, but necessary.

She didn't soften the message but she delivered it with care and reverence. She honoured God, and in doing so, helped guide a king and his people back to the covenant they had long neglected.

Huldah's story reminds us that prophetic voices are not always thunderous. Sometimes, they are quiet, precise, and rooted in deep listening. In a world full of noise, Huldah encourages us to cultivate hearts tuned to God's Word — and when called, to speak with clarity and courage.

A Sister's Light

"She never sought a crowd to affirm her worth. Praise and adoration were never her aim. Her wisdom dwelled in quiet places, and in time, through the sharing of her experiences, reflections, and meditations through her writings, her truth found a home in the hearts of many."

Journaling Invitations

1.   When have you been called to speak a truth that was difficult but important? What helped you find your voice?

2.   How do you seek God's guidance when you face moments of decision or uncertainty?

3.   Are there "scrolls" in your life: truths or callings, that have been set aside and might be waiting to be rediscovered?

4.   Reflect on a time when someone's quiet wisdom made a lasting impact on you. What did it stir in your own heart?

Next is the Shunammite woman's story. This is a one of quiet generosity, deep faith, and unwavering trust in the face of both joy and sorrow. Her life reminds us of the strength found in hospitality, resilience, and hope. Let us now turn to her story.

The Shunammite Woman: A Heart Open to God

2 Kings 4:8–37; 2 Kings 8:1–6

The Story

In the hill country of Shunem lived a woman whose name we are never told ... only that she was "a prominent woman." What we do know is this: she was thoughtful, generous, and spiritually perceptive.

One day, the prophet Elisha passed through her town, and she invited him in for a meal. Sensing he was a holy man of God, she spoke to her husband and suggested they build a small upper room ... a place for Elisha to rest whenever he travelled through.

Her kindness was quiet but profound. She asked for nothing. But Elisha, moved by her hospitality, wanted to bless her. Through the word of the Lord, he told her that though she had no son and her husband was old, she would bear a child.

And she did.

Years later, the boy (her miracle child) suddenly collapsed in the fields and died in her arms. With calm but determined faith, she laid him on Elisha's bed and set out to find the prophet.

When Elisha saw her coming, he could see she was deeply troubled. But she said only, "It is well." She clung to him with the grief of a mother and the faith of one who still believed.

Elisha returned with her, entered the room, and prayed. After a sacred and mysterious moment, the child opened his eyes and the Shunammite woman fell at Elisha's feet in gratitude.

Later, she would heed Elisha's warning to leave the land during a famine. Upon her return seven years later, she approached the king to ask for her home. At that very moment, Elisha's servant was telling the king her story. The king restored everything she had lost; a full circle of grace.

Reflection

The Shunammite woman's story shines with steadfastness. She is not loud or dramatic. She moves with quiet strength, trusting in God without needing to understand every step.

She opens her home to the prophet without expectation. She opens her heart to the promise of a son, even after years of silence. And when tragedy comes, she does not panic — she seeks God.

Even in heartbreak, she says, *"It is well."* Not because the pain is small, but because her trust is great.

Her story teaches us that hospitality is holy. That spiritual perception is a gift. That miracles do not always mean a life without sorrow but rather, a life lived in constant dialogue with the Divine.

In every chapter of her life, the Shunammite woman lives with openness; to God's word, God's people, and God's timing.

A Sister's Light

"Her hands made space for others; her heart made space for hope. And when the shadows came, she did not close the door; she went straight to the Giver of Life. She was ready."

Journaling Invitations

1. Where are you being called to make space ... in your home, your heart, your schedule ... for the presence of God or others?

2. Have you ever experienced a time when things fell apart, yet something inside you whispered, "It is well"?

3. Write about a time when quiet generosity or faithfulness brought unexpected blessings.

4. What would it mean for you today to walk in the Shunammite woman's kind of trust ... one that seeks, believes, and endures?

For our final story, we look at Mary Magdalene ... a name that echoes with depth, grace, and transformation. Her story is one of healing, profound love, and faithful witness. Though often misunderstood, she is a symbol of redemption and the transformative power of encountering Christ. Let us now, reflect on her life.

Carole Somerville

Mary Magdalene: A Woman Transformed by Love

Luke 8:1–3; John 19:25–27; John 20:1–18

The Story

Mary Magdalene's story begins in the shadows of pain. The Gospels tell us that Jesus healed her from seven demons ... an affliction that would have left her isolated, rejected, and in deep despair. But when she met Jesus, everything changed. He cast out her demons, healed her, and restored her to wholeness.

Mary became one of Jesus' most devoted followers. She was present in the many moments of Jesus' ministry, travelling with Him and the other women who supported Him. She witnessed His miracles, heard His words, and felt the weight of His love.

At the cross, while many of His disciples had fled in fear, Mary Magdalene remained — standing by Him in His suffering. She watched as His body was taken down, and she prepared to honour Him in death.

But it was at the tomb that the true depth of Mary's love and devotion would be revealed. Early on the first day of the week, she came to the tomb and found it empty. Overcome with grief, she wept. As she turned around, she encountered a man she thought was the gardener, until He spoke her name: "Mary." And in that moment, the risen Jesus stood before her.

Mary's response was immediate: "Rabboni!" (a term of endearment, meaning "my teacher.") She wanted to cling to Him, but Jesus told her, "Do not hold on to me, for I have not yet ascended to the Father." Yet He gave her a special mission: "Go to my brothers and tell them, 'I am ascending to my Father and your Father, to my God and your God.'"

Mary became the first to witness the resurrection, the first to carry the good news to the disciples. She is known as the "Apostle to the Apostles" because she was entrusted with proclaiming Christ's victory over death.

Reflection

Mary Magdalene's story is one of profound transformation. From being bound by darkness to being set free by the light of Christ, she is a picture of what it means to be redeemed ... to be seen, known, and loved by God.

Her faithfulness at the cross, her grief at the tomb, and her joy at the resurrection all reveal her heart: a heart of love, deep devotion, and courage. She didn't just follow Jesus from a distance. She stayed close, even in His darkest hour, and when she found the tomb empty, her love led her to search for Him. And when she encountered the risen Christ, she responded in worship.

Mary Magdalene reminds us that Christ's love transforms us completely. No one is beyond redemption. We are not defined by our past or by the struggles we face, but by the grace that Jesus extends to us. When we encounter Him, we too can be transformed, called by name, and sent to share the good news.

Her encounter with the risen Christ is a powerful reminder that in our moments of sorrow, grief, or confusion, Jesus sees us and He calls us by name. He doesn't just give us hope; He gives us Himself.

For the non-religious: Mary Magdalene's journey reminds us that love has the power to transform us completely. No one is beyond healing or renewal. We are not defined by our past or the challenges we face, but by the grace that is offered to us. When we encounter this love, we too can be transformed, called with purpose, and invited to share hope with others. Her encounter with the risen presence is a profound reminder that in our moments of sorrow, grief, or confusion, we are seen ... and called by name. It is not just hope that we are given, but the very presence of love that holds us.

A Sister's Light

"She lingered in the shadow of grief and pain, and in a single moment, the moment she had been waiting for, she was called into the light. Her heart beat with the certainty of love that would never fade."

Journaling Invitations

1.   Christians: What does it mean to you to be seen and known by Christ? How has His love transformed your life?

2.   Reflect on a time when you experienced grief or sorrow, and Christ/the Divine met you in that place.

3.   How can you share a message of hope and renewal in your life today, as Mary Magdalene shared her experience with the disciples?

4.   Write a reflection of gratitude, acknowledging those times when you felt deeply understood and how they have transformed your perspective and heart.

☽✦ Handwritten Reflections ✦☽

You are invited to sit quietly with what you've read. Below is space for your own thoughts, prayers, or dreams that rise as you ponder these bible stories and their meaning in your life.

✦ *"The heavens declare the glory of God; the skies proclaim the work of His hands." — Psalm 19:1* ✦
Let these pages be your sacred sky.

Thank you for joining me on this journey through this book. Whether you come from a Christian perspective or have been exploring these stories from other viewpoints, I hope these reflections have offered something meaningful and enriching for you.

Carole Anne

Printed in Great Britain
by Amazon